A Pilgrim's Journey

The Autobiography
of
Ignatius of Loyola

*Introduction, Translation and Commentary
by
Joseph N. Tylenda, S.J.*

A Michael Glazier Book
THE LITURGICAL PRESS
Collegeville, Minnesota

A Michael Glazier Book published by The Liturgical Press

Cover by Placid Stuckenschneider, O.S.B.

	3	4	5	6	7	8	9

To
Youree and Alexander
Joseph, Paul, and Anthony
Best of Friends and
Beloved Brothers in the Priesthood

Contents

Appendices

Introduction

I. "The Pilgrim's Journey"

Sometime during the year 1552, two of Ignatius Loyola's closest associates, Juan de Polanco and Jerónimo Nadal, made a special request of him.[1] Now that Ignatius had finished writing the Constitutions of the Society of Jesus, and since Ignatius' health had been growing progressively worse, both friends feared that they would not long have their beloved Founder with them, and thus they asked him to leave his followers "some admonition as a testament," which would show them the way to virtue. Other founders of religious Orders had done this,[2] and Polanco and Nadal thought it behooved Ignatius to do the same. With this in mind, Nadal approached Ignatius and requested him to narrate how God had guided him from the first days of his conversion until the present. To Nadal's way of thinking, such a description of the divine action in Ignatius' soul would at the same time describe the founding of the Society of Jesus.

Ignatius was reluctant to yield to their request—he was always unwilling to talk about himself. Though his colleagues continued to urge him to compose this testament, Ignatius procrastinated and changed his mind only after Luis Gonçalves da Câmara had met him in the garden adjacent to their Roman residence, on August 4, 1553, and had spoken with him. Gonçalves da Câmara was a Portuguese, born about 1519, and the son of the governor of Madeira. In 1535 he went to Paris to study languages and philosophy, and there met Peter Faber and the other companions and manifested an interest in their enterprise. Ignatius had already left Paris for his return visit to Spain. After concluding his studies, Gonçalves da Câmara returned to Portugal and entered the Society in Lisbon on April 27, 1545. In 1553, he was summoned to Rome to report on the Society in Portugal and arrived in the Eternal City on May 23. In Rome he was appointed minister of the Jesuit residence and remained there until October 23, 1555, when he returned to Portugal.[3]

In their chat in the garden, Gonçalves da Câmara spoke to Ignatius about vainglory, and while Ignatius was telling him the means to overcome it, Ignatius' thoughts took him back to his own pre-conversion days when vanity dictated his every action. Perhaps the sixty-two-year-old Ignatius saw himself in the thirty-four-year-old Luis struggling against vanity, and while Polanco and Nadal had been unsuccessful in their attempt to get Ignatius to reveal his interior life to them, this Portuguese Jesuit unknowingly succeeded. Ignatius realized that if he were to narrate the journey he had made from being a vain courtier to a humble pilgrim seeking only God, it would not only help Gonçalves da Câmara to overcome his present inclination to vainglory, but it might also help others. Thus, Ignatius chose him as the one to whom he would describe his pilgrim journey.

Ignatius began the narration of his life's story toward the end of August 1553, just a couple of weeks after he had made the decision to do so. Though Gonçalves da Câmara states in his Preface that Ignatius dictated this material, he does not mean to say that he was an amanuensis, there and then recording each and every word Ignatius uttered. During Ignatius' narration he listened attentively, but only after he had left Ignatius and had gone to his room did he jot down, in brief or outline form, what he had heard. Some time later—was it days or weeks?—he enfleshed these notes of his and read them to a Spanish scribe who then recorded them verbatim. Gonçalves da Câmara insists in his Preface that he tried "not to write a single word other than those that I have heard from the Father,"[4] and Nadal assures us in his Preface that Gonçalves da Câmara was "endowed with an excellent memory."[5] Even with such an excellent memory there are a few inconsistencies between what Gonçalves da Câmara wrote in his Preface and what is found in the text itself.[6]

Ignatius interrupted his narration sometime in September 1553, having reached, at that time, his first days in Manresa. This interruption lasted seventeen months, and it was only on March 9, 1555, that he again returned to telling his story, but then, due to the death of Pope Julius III on March 23, the narration was again delayed. This second interruption lasted six months. Since Ignatius decided on September 21, 1555, that Gonçalves da Câmara was to return to Spain, there was now some urgency for him to conclude what he had begun. Gonçalves da Câmara met with him on September 22 and continued until October 20 (according to the text) or October 22 (according to the Preface). The material collected during this third period of narration remained in the form of abbreviated notes until Gonçalves da Câmara arrived in Genoa in November 1555. While waiting for passage to Spain, he took the notes he had made the month before, prepared them, and dictated the remainder of the text to an Italian scribe, since no Spanish scribe was available. Thus, the first two thirds of the text were written in Spanish and the final third in Italian.

The text covers but eighteen of Ignatius' sixty-five years. It begins with his wounding at the siege of Pamplona (1521), and describes his conversion at Loyola, his growth in the spiritual life through the extraordinary graces he received at Manresa, his pilgrimage to the Holy Land, his decision to study and his life in Barcelona, Alcalá, Salamanca, and Paris. Finally, unable to go to the Holy Land, Ignatius and his companions went to Rome to place themselves at the disposal of the pope (1538). Ignatius' first thirty years, that is, his youth and life as a courtier, are not included in the text, but a resumé of that portion of his life is given in Part II of this Introduction. Likewise, the remaining seventeen years of his life in

Rome as Father General of a new religious Order are outside the text and are treated in Part III of this Introduction.

The text that Gonçalves da Câmara had dictated to the two Spanish scribes in Rome, and the Italian scribe in Genoa, is not extant; however, several copies of that Spanish-Italian text had been made at a very early date, for Nadal had such a copy and had carried it with him on his visit to the various Jesuit houses. Sometime between 1558 and 1561, Father Annibal du Coudret, a Frenchman then stationed in Rome, translated the Spanish-Italian text into Latin, and since Nadal appears to have been unaware that Gonçalves da Câmara had written a preface to the text, he wrote his own (see Appendix I); since the text was without a title, Nadal gave it one, calling it *The Acts of Father Ignatius, as Father Luis Gonçalves First Wrote Them, Receiving Them from the Mouth of the Father Himself.*

Du Coudret's Latin translation of the text was the first to be published in the *Acta Sanctorum*, vol. VII *Julii* (1731). The Spanish-Italian text was first published only in 1904, in the *Monumenta Ignatiana: Scripta de Sancto Ignatio de Loyola* 1 (Madrid). This was the first critical edition; another critical edition, together with du Coudret's Latin translation, appeared in *Fontes Narrativi de S. Ignatio de Loyola* 1: *Narrationes scriptae ante annum 1557* (Rome: Monumenta Historica Societatis Iesu, 1943). This edition, together with that of Candido de Dalmases, S.I., in *Obras Completas de San Ignacio de Loyola* (Madrid: Biblioteca de Autores Cristianos, 1982), provide the basis for our present English translation.

To date five English translations have appeared. In 1900 two were published almost simultaneously: that of E. M. Rix, *The Testament of Ignatius Loyola* (London), and that of J. F. X. O'Conor, S.J., *The Autobiography of St. Ignatius* (New York: Benziger). Both these translations were made prior to the publication of the critical Spanish-Italian text and relied exclusively on du Coudret's Latin version in the *Acta Sanctorum*. All subsequent translations have been based on the critical text. In 1956 William J. Young, S.J., offered his translation, calling it *St. Ignatius' Own Story: As Told to Luis González de Cámara* (Chicago: Regnery); and in 1974 there followed *The Autobiography of St. Ignatius Loyola* (New York: Harper & Row), translated by Joseph F. O'Callaghan. The most recent is that of Parmananda R. Divarkar, *A Pilgrim's Testament: The Memoirs of Ignatius of Loyola* (Rome: Gregorian University, 1983).

With these several translations, why another one? Inasmuch as the story that Ignatius tells is brief, compact, and somewhat incomplete, the text really calls for a commentary which Ignatius' contemporaries would certainly have been able to supply but not so the modern reader. Furthermore, a commentary is needed to explain the various allusions in the text, to clarify some of its ambiguities and, in general, to give the reader a fuller flowing biographical sketch of the Founder of the Jesuits and thus to be a complement to the text. Since a commentary was therefore deemed necessary, a new translation was prepared at the same time, for only by wrestling with the Spanish-Italian text does one come close to Ignatius and become better equipped to write a commentary. The commentary that follows is heavily dependent upon the abundant historical data supplied by Candido de Dalmases, S.I., both in his 1943 critical edition and in his 1982 edition.

Since Gonçalves da Câmara had never given a title to the text he produced, it remained for later editors and translators to add their own. As previously noted, Nadal called it the *Acts of Ignatius*, since it delineated Ignatius' life and deeds over a period of eighteen years. Both O'Conor and O'Callaghan have called it Ignatius' *Autobiography*, and such it is, since Ignatius narrated his life history. Young paraphrases that idea and calls it *Ignatius' Own Story*. Rix calls it Ignatius' *Testament*, since this was what Nadal and Polanco had requested of him, and Divarkar calls it *A Pilgrim's Testament*, joining the fact that this was Ignatius' testament to his sons and the fact that in the text Ignatius always refers to himself in the third person and frequently calls himself "the pilgrim."

I have entitled this translation *The Pilgrim's Journey*, taking into account that "pilgrim" is what Ignatius had called himself and that throughout his life he was on a pilgrimage seeking God. The journey he made during those years was not merely a land/sea journey to the Holy Land and through Europe; more importantly, it was a spiritual journey that he had embarked upon. After his conversion, Ignatius sought God and God alone. He left Loyola in order to seek God in the Holy Land, and he ends his narration saying that now "at whatever time or hour he wants to find God, he finds Him."

In the present edition the translation of Gonçalves da Câmara's text appears on the upper portion of the page while the commentary is on the lower portion. The numbering of the paragraphs coincides in text and commentary.

II. Early Life of Ignatius Loyola, 1491-1520

Ignatius, the seventh and youngest son of Beltrán Ibáñez de Oñaz y Loyola and Marina Sánchez de Licona, was born in the family castle in Azpeitia, in the Basque province of Guipúzcoa in northern Spain. He was baptized in the parish church of San Sebastián de Soreasu and was given the name Iñigo López. Iñigo was a common name among the Basques and it recalled the saintly Benedictine Abbot of Oña, who died in 1057; the López part of his name derived from one of his ancestors. For the first forty-four years of his life he was known as Iñigo, and only in 1535, when he received his master's diploma at the University of Paris, did he become Ignatius. It seems that the university officials, unaware that the Latin form of Iñigo was *Enecus*, Latinized his Basque name into *Ignatius*, and since that time Iñigo has been known as Master Ignatius.

The recognized year of Ignatius' birth is 1491, but since his baptismal record was destroyed by fire, the exact date of his birth is lost to history. In narrating the events of his life to Gonçalves da Câmara, Ignatius said (#1) that he was twenty-six at the time of the siege of Pamplona (1521), which would mean that he was born in 1495. The text later states (#30) that he was sixty-two years old in 1555, which would then have him born in 1493. When the early Jesuits attempted to solve this discrepancy and approached the woman who had nursed him in infancy, they asked her whether Ignatius actually was sixty-two in 1555. The woman immediately corrected them, saying that Ignatius was two years older, meaning that he had been born in 1491.[7] Since the woman was already advanced in years there was the possibility that her memory might have been faulty. But many years later a legal document, drawn up by a notary in Azpeitia, was happily discovered. The document is dated October 23, 1505, and mentions that Iñigo of Loyola acted as a witness in the sale of a horse.[8] Since the law of Castile and Guipúzcoa stipulates that no male who had not passed his fourteenth birthday could validly act as a witness in a legal matter, it then follows that our Iñigo of Loyola was born sometime prior to October 23, 1491.

Besides his six brothers Ignatius also had three sisters, and there were perhaps three other offspring of his father, but Ignatius was the youngest of all.[9] Since he had been given to María de Garín, the young wife of a blacksmith living a short distance from the castle, to be nursed, it is generally presumed that Ignatius' mother had died when he was still an infant.[10] It is not known how long he lived with his nurse, nor is it known when he returned to live with his family in the castle. Since Juan Pérez, Ignatius' oldest brother, had died in 1496 during the Spanish campaign in Naples, Martín García, the second son, became heir to the family estate. Martín García married Magdalena de Araoz on September 11, 1498,[11] and since he brought his wife home to be the new mistress of Loyola, this may have been as good a time as any for Ignatius to return to his ancestral residence. Ignatius' education at Loyola was minimal according to today's standards, but according to those of that age it was deemed quite satisfactory, for he knew how to read and write.

Among Ignatius' father's friends was Juan Velázquez de Cuéllar, King Ferdinand's chief treasurer, whose wife, Maria Velasco, was related to Ignatius' mother. Velázquez wrote to Ignatius' father, perhaps sometime in 1506, suggesting that the elder Loyola might want to send one of his younger sons to live with Velázquez at Arévalo and be educated as a Castilian gentleman. Velázquez' invitation was readily accepted and the father chose to send the fifteen-year-old Ignatius to Arévalo, some 400 miles away. Together with Velázquez' sons, Ignatius was trained in courtly manners and learned riding and fencing, dancing and singing, and all that was expected of a courtier. It was also at Arévalo that he was introduced to the literature of the day—the adventure-filled novels of chivalry. As the king's treasurer, Velázquez was frequently at court and often had to travel with it when it went to Madrid or Segovia, Valladolid or Medina del Campo. As Ignatius grew older and became more accustomed to courtly life, he too was included in Velázquez' retinue.

From Ignatius' eleven or so years with Velázquez, only one incident has come down to us. Ignatius made periodic visits to Loyola—his father had already died in 1507—but his visit in February 1515 became the occasion of a legal action against him. The Loyola family was the patron of the church of San Sebastián de Soreasu in Azpeitia, whose rector was Juan de Anchieta. Until 1515 Anchieta had been Master of the Chapel Royal, and during that time he lived at court, leaving the parish in the care of his vicars. But Anchieta now returned to Azpeitia and thought about retiring. As the church's patron, the Loyola family had the right to appoint Anchieta's successor and the family intended to grant the benefice to their priest-brother, Pero López. Disregarding the Loyolas' right to make the new appointment, Anchieta went ahead and named his nephew, García López de Anchieta, to succeed him. On Shrove Tuesday, February 20, 1515, Ignatius, Pero López, and several others, taking advantage of the fact that it was carnival time, became involved in some sort of harassment or violence directed against the parish clergy in Azpeitia. Whatever happened that evening was considered to be sufficiently serious for a legal action was introduced against Ignatius, the presumed ringleader. Some of the documents of that process are extant,[12] but none of them mentions the actual charge brought against Ignatius. Nevertheless, in the eyes of the magistrate it was considered to have been "very serious," since it had been perpetrated "during the night, with malice aforethought, and treacherously carried out by means of an ambush."[13]

In response to this legal action, both brothers, Pero López and Ignatius, appealed to clerical immunity. This was possible since Pero López was a priest and Ignatius had received the tonsure. The brothers thus claimed that they had the right to be tried by an ecclesiastical and not a secular court. It is not known when Ignatius had received the tonsure for there is no record of it in the Pamplona diocesan archives, but it must have been sometime prior to his going to Arévalo to serve as Velázquez' page. To enjoy clerical immunity, Ignatius would have had to have worn the tonsure and clerical dress for four months immediately preceding the crime. But it was common knowledge in Azpeitia that Ignatius' tonsure was much smaller than the prescribed size and that he always dressed in slashed suits of bright colors with flowing cape, and wore tight-fitting colored hose and boots. A sword and dagger were at his waist, his long curly hair rested on his shoulders, and his cap proudly sported a feather. Furthermore, he was frequently seen wearing a breastplate and coat of mail. It was the magistrate's opinion that since Ignatius decked himself out in the finery of a secular soldier and not in the somber colors of the heavenly militia, he should stand trial before the secular court.[14]

The case against Ignatius seems to have been eventually dropped, for there are no extant documents explaining how it ended. But the knowledge of the scandal he once caused in Azpeitia remained with him, and in 1535, when he returned to his native land to recuperate, Ignatius chose to live in Azpeitia and beg his daily bread, thus making reparation for his earlier unbecoming behavior.

King Ferdinand died on January 23, 1516, but prior to his death he had appointed his sixteen-year-old grandson, Charles, to act as regent for his unfortunate mother, Queen Juana la Loca. Charles was to succeed to the throne upon his mother's death, but rather than wait for nature to have its course, Charles had himself declared king on March 14, 1516, in Flanders, and then changed the provisions in his grandfather's will. While Ferdinand left a pension for his second wife, Germaine de Foix, from monies coming from Naples, Charles ordered that the money was to come from certain Castilian towns, including Arévalo and others directly under Velázquez' authority. The citizens of these cities, and Velázquez with them, expressed their surprise and displeasure, especially since the cities had been granted the privilege of nonalienation from the Castilian crown. According to Charles' decision, these towns would now belong to Queen Germaine, who in fact was a foreigner and the niece of the King of France. The result was that Velázquez was removed from office; he moved to Madrid and there he died a broken man on August 12, 1517.

With Velázquez' death, Ignatius had to seek new employment. Growing sated with the life of a courtier, he now thought of following that of a soldier, seeking renown by gallantry in battle. Ignatius thus entered the service of Don Antonio Manrique de Lara, Duke of Nájera and Viceroy of Navarre. In September 1520, when the townspeople of Nájera were engaged in a minor revolt against their duke, Ignatius played a major part in bringing the city back to the duke's obedience. And when there was a minor disturbance in Guipúzcoa, between the cities of San Sebastián and Hernani, the duke sent Ignatius there to bring peace to that region, which he succeeded in doing. It was while Ignatius was in Guipúzcoa that the duke urgently sent for him to return since the French were advancing on Pamplona. Ignatius and his men rushed toward the Navarrese capital and the events that followed his arrival form the beginning of the story that Ignatius narrated to Gonçalves da Câmara.

III. Later Life of Ignatius Loyola, 1539-1556

Ignatius' narration to Gonçalves da Câmara ends with the year 1538. He had then been in Rome for a whole year, and since he and his companions were unable to go to the Holy Land and there labor for souls, they offered their service to Pope Paul III in November 1538. They had banded together with the express purpose of converting the infidel, but now that that goal was impossible to attain, the group was faced with a vexing problem. Should they disband, or should they remain together? If they were to remain as a group, should they remain as they were, that is, a group bound by mutual charity and dedicated to the salvation of souls, or should they form themselves into a religious congregation and, in addition to their vows of poverty and chastity, should they take a vow to obey the individual who would be elected as their head?

With this in mind, these first Jesuits gathered in Rome in mid-March 1539 and began a series of discussions. Up to now they had never given any thought to the possibility of forming a new congregation in the Church. Their deliberations lasted through Lent and a good part of the Easter season. By April 15 they unanimously decided to remain together and to form

a new congregation with the vow of obedience. Discussion
continued until June 24, touching on questions as to the
nature of their new organization, its purpose and function,
whether they should undertake the running of colleges and
churches, how new members should be added, etc. Ignatius
was deputed to summarize these discussions in a document
that would eventually be presented to the pope. By the end
of June or early July, Ignatius had completed his task, and that
summary has come to be known as the Formula of the Institute.[15] Ignatius then requested Cardinal Contarini to sub-
mit it to the pope for his approval. The cardinal read the document to Pope Paul III on September 3, and His Holiness immediately approved it, saying that these priests would be of
great help in the reform of the Church.[16] The pope then
directed that the official bull approving the Society of Jesus be
prepared and promulgated.

The papal bull *Regimini militantis Ecclesiae*, granting official
approval to the Society, was not published until a year had
passed, that is, on September 27, 1540. While the Jesuits were
waiting for this approbation they continued their usual
preaching and teaching, hearing confessions and catechizing.
Faber and Laínez had gone to northern Italy to rekindle the
faith among the Parmesans, and Rodrigues and Xavier had left
for Portugal. Since the Society of Jesus had been officially and
canonically recognized by the Holy See, it now had to draw
up Constitutions in accord with the apostolate described in the
Formula and approved in the papal bull. The companions who
were then in Rome met on March 4, 1541, and agreed that
the task of writing the Constitutions should be given to Ignatius and that Codure was to assist him. There was also the
question of choosing one of their number as general and so Ignatius asked all who could conveniently come to Rome to be
there for the middle of Lent. Those who were unable to come
because of distance were to send their vote in writing. Of the
original companions, four were unable to attend: Faber was

in Germany, Rodrigues and Xavier were in Portugal, and Bobadilla in Calabria. The remaining six decided that before voting they should spend three days in prayer and only at the end of that period should they write down their choice for general. After these three days their votes were placed in a box together with those that had been received from those companions who were unable to come. They waited another three days and then on April 8, 1541, the ballots were read. Each was a vote for Ignatius; his own ballot showed that he had voted for "the one whom the majority would elect."

Ignatius declined the election, insisting that since he could not govern himself, he was unable to govern others; that the sins of his past life weighed so heavily upon him that he could not take on so important a role; and, finally, that he preferred to obey rather than to command. But his entreaty met deaf ears. He then asked his companions to consider the matter prayerfully for another three days. The second ballot was cast on April 13 and it confirmed the previous one, but Ignatius was still reluctant to accept, and so he asked for several days in which to pray and seek advice from his Franciscan confessor. Ignatius then went to the Franciscan monastery of San Pietro in Montorio, on Rome's Janiculum, and after days of intense prayer and consultation with his confessor, the advice he received was that he had to accept the office of general of the Society since this was the manifest will of God. Ignatius accepted the election on April 19 and on the 22nd—it was Friday of Easter Week—he and his five companions set out to visit the seven ancient churches of Rome. When they finally arrived at St. Paul Outside-the-Walls, they made their confessions to each other, and as Ignatius celebrated Mass in the Chapel of Our Lady these six Jesuits, at the moment of Communion, pronounced their vows in the newly formed Society of Jesus.

At the time of his election as general, Ignatius was fifty years old. His contemporaries have described him as being somewhat small in stature but sturdily built, and as walking with a limp because of the wound he had received at Pamplona. His face was round, with a pointed chin; his nose was aquiline and he had a high smooth forehead with a hairline that receded with age. His eyes were said to have been deepset and cheerful; his hair was brown, with a touch of grey in it, and he kept his beard short and trimmed after the manner of the masters at the University of Paris.[17]

Ignatius had fifteen years in which to form and guide the new Society. Besides overseeing its growth and development, he spent a good part of these years writing and perfecting the Society's Constitutions. Ignatius also carried on an extensive correspondence, not only concerning what was necessary for the everyday business of the Society, but also as guidance to many individuals in the ways of the spiritual life. The Society did not limit its activity to Rome; Ignatius sent his Jesuits wherever bishops had need of them. Whether it was to northern or southern Italy, France or Germany, Spain or Portugal, the Jesuits went to instruct the people in the faith and to give the Spiritual Exercises to all whom they judged ready. These Jesuits carried God's word from city to city, and so successfully that within a few years of its foundation the Society had houses in the major cities of Europe. From these fruitful contacts a continuous stream of candidates for the Society made its way to Rome, among them Peter Canisius and Francis Borgia. As Jesuit influence increased in these cities, colleges were opened and so rapid was the Society's growth that by 1556, the year of Ignatius' death, it totaled 1,000 members in seventy-six houses in twelve provinces, including Brazil, Japan, and India.

Ignatius began writing the Constitutions in 1541; though the process may have been slow, it was, nevertheless, thorough. By 1548 he saw himself nearing the end and so he asked the professed fathers to come to Rome, and during December 1550 and January 1551 he submitted the Constitutions to their scrutiny and asked for their observations. The fathers heartily approved what had been shown them, and Ignatius recognized that in places the text had to be clarified or expanded. Standing before these same fathers, Ignatius, on January 30, 1551, humbly asked to resign his office as general, citing his numerous sins, imperfections, and infirmities which, in his judgment, prevented him from governing the Society as he felt it should be governed.[18] But the Jesuits gathered in Rome refused to accept the resignation and begged him, for the good of the Society, to continue bearing the burden of government.

In 1551 Ignatius established the Roman College, which he wanted to be the model for all Jesuit colleges throughout the world. To help counteract the growing influence of the Reformation in Germany, he established in 1552 a college in Rome for German seminarians so that they could be properly and thoroughly trained for the work that would be demanded of them on their return to their homeland. Ignatius was likewise attuned to the needs of Rome. He founded the House of Saint Martha for former prostitutes and a home for young girls who were especially in danger of being exploited, and he established an orphanage and had a house made ready for Moors and Jews who had expressed a desire to become Christians.

Ever since his Paris days, Ignatius had suffered from stomach ailments; these were especially troublesome during the last ten years of his life. As his work increased, especially his concern about the Society's Constitutions, his health declined. There were months during 1554 and 1555 when he was unable to leave his sick bed. In the winter of 1555-1556 he found new strength, but by April he was again failing. The Roman summer of 1556 was oppressive and since Ignatius was not improving his physician recommended that he go to the villa on the Aventine. This he did on July 2. The air there, however, was no more salubrious than that of the city and so on July 24 he returned to the residence in the center of Rome. So intense was the heat that several Jesuits at the residence also fell ill with fever. When the physician came to examine these sick Jesuits he also checked on Ignatius, but the Founder was neither better nor worse, and since he had survived similar bouts in the past the physician was sure that he would survive this one as well. Ignatius, however, thought differently.

On Thursday, July 30, Ignatius called his secretary, Polanco, to his bedside and asked him to go to the Vatican that afternoon to request the pope's blessing for him, to recommend the Society to his good will, and to assure him that if, by God's mercy, he were admitted into heaven, his prayer for the Vicar of Christ would be all the more fervent. Although Ignatius was suggesting that his death was imminent, Polanco put more trust in the physician's statement that he would recover. And so he informed Ignatius that since he had several letters that had to be written and sent to Spain that day, he would go to the Vatican on the following day. Ignatius intimated that he would prefer Polanco to go that afternoon; nevertheless, he told him, "Do as you wish." Polanco returned to his letters. Later, when Polanco was with Ignatius for the evening meal, they chatted as usual and, sure that he had made the right decision, Polanco went peacefully to bed.

Shortly after midnight, Ignatius took a turn for the worse. When the infirmarian checked on him at daybreak, it was clear that he was in his last moments. The brother hurriedly called several priests to the Founder's room, and Polanco rushed off to the Vatican to secure the papal blessing. But before he returned Ignatius, the one-time soldier who had become a pilgrim for the love of Christ, had given his soul to God. The news of his death brought many to the Jesuit residence, and when the body was made ready for viewers, there was a long line of cardinals and priests, of Rome's nobility and Rome's poor, all coming to kiss the venerable hands of the Founder of the Society of Jesus. On Saturday evening, August 1, he was buried in the church of Our Lady della Strada, and when that edifice was replaced by the magnificent church of the Gesú, his remains were interred there in 1587.

Ignatius Loyola was beatified by Pope Paul V on July 27, 1609, and was canonized by Pope Gregory XV on March 12, 1622.

Feast of All Saints and Blessed
of the Society of Jesus

Preface
of
Father Luis Gonçalves da Câmara

1. One Friday morning, August 4, the vigil of Our Lady of the Snows, in the year 1553, while the Father was in the garden near the house or apartment known as that of the duke, I began giving him an account of some matters pertaining to my soul, and I spoke to him, among other things, about vainglory. As a remedy the Father counseled me to frequently refer all my affairs to God, to aim at offering Him all the good that I find in myself, to acknowledge that these are all His gifts, and to thank Him for them. He spoke to me about these matters in such a way that I was greatly consoled and as a result I could not hold back my tears. The Father then told me how for two years he had struggled against this vice and with such

1. Luis Gonçalves da Câmara[1] was a Portuguese Jesuit who had come to Rome in 1553, and had been appointed minister (assistant to the superior) in the community where Ignatius lived. He had been in Rome only two months and held the Founder of the Society in such esteem that throughout this Preface he refers to Ignatius as "the Father." When he met with Ignatius in the garden near the duke's apartment—so called because Francis Borgia, when still Duke of Gandía, stayed there while visiting Rome during the Holy Year of 1550-1551—Ignatius was sixty-two years old and had but three more years to live. Because pilgrims going to the Holy Land were greatly respected by the faithful and at times were even regarded as saintly individuals, Ignatius deliberately kept reticent about his trip. He feared that if he were to reveal his plans, others would show him undeserved honor,

effort that when he was about to set sail from Barcelona for Jerusalem he dared not tell anyone that he was going to Jerusalem, and he did the same in other circumstances. He added, with regard to this matter, that great peace of soul was his ever afterwards.

An hour or two later we were at dinner, and while Master Polanco and I were eating with him, our Father said that many times Master Nadal and others of the Society had made a special request of him, but he had never come to any decision about it. Now, after having spoken with me, and having gone to his room, he felt a powerful inclination and desire to fulfill that request, and — speaking in such a way that it was clear that God had inspired him to see what his duty was — he was now determined to do it, that is, narrate all that had happened in his soul up to the present time, and he likewise decided that I was to be the one to whom he would reveal these matters.

2. At that time the Father was very ill, and was not in the habit of promising himself even a single day more. In fact, whenever anyone said: "I'll do that two weeks hence," or "a

---

and rather than expose himself to any temptation toward vanity he kept his projected pilgrimage a secret.

Later that day, while at dinner, Ignatius mentioned that some members of the Society — and among these were Polanco[2] and Nadal[3] — had asked him to leave an account of the way that God had worked in his soul, leading him to conversion and to the founding of the Society of Jesus. This request was first made of Ignatius in 1552,[4] but up to August 1553 he had done nothing about it. Now, after the day's conversation in the garden, he realized that if he were to narrate his life it would not be an exercise in vanity but an exercise in humility. He would not be relating his own accomplishments but God's wondrous actions in him. If what he had told Gonçalves da Câmara had been helpful, perhaps the same would be helpful to others as well, and thus he decided to grant the request made of him.

2. Though Ignatius had come to the decision to narrate his life in early August 1553, Gonçalves da Câmara's Preface seems to indicate that the narration began in September of that year. He here differs from what he says in #10 of the text, where he writes that that part was written in August 1553. Perhaps when writing his Preface he did not take the time to read

week from today," the Father, somewhat surprised, always said: "What's that? Do you think you will live that long?" Nevertheless, on this occasion, he said that he hoped to live for three or four months so that he could complete this task. In speaking to him the following day I asked when he would like us to begin, and he replied that every day I should remind him of it (I can't recall how many days!), until he felt ready to do so. Not having the time because of pressing duties, he wanted me to remind him of it every Sunday. Thus, in September (I don't remember the date), the Father called me and began to tell me about his entire life, as well as his youthful escapades, and all this clearly and distinctly and in full detail. Later in the same month he called me three or four times and carried his story up to his first days in Manresa, as one can see by the difference in the writing.

what he had previously written and merely meant to say that the first portion was completed during September of that year. Altogether he had four or five meetings (August-September) with Ignatius before the first major interruption came. How much material was covered during those meetings? The Preface says that Ignatius got as far as his first days in Manresa and that the difference in the handwriting in the text—where one scribe ended and another began—would indicate the place where the first meetings ended.

It would be nice to pinpoint the exact place in the text where that interruption occurred, but since the writer's original manuscript is lost, and only copies remain, there is no way of examining the difference in scribal penmanship. But the mention of Ignatius' first days in Manresa is a help. Since Ignatius experienced his singular illumination on the banks of the Cardoner river some months after his arrival in Manresa (#30-31), it would then seem that the first talks ended somewhere between #19 and #30.

During these meetings Ignatius likewise described the various escapades of his youth, and this was not a mere mention of them, but they were told with all their details. These capers, however, are not included in the text as it has come down to us. Were they in the original manuscript now lost? If so, then why were they deleted when copies were made? If not in the original manuscript, was it because Ignatius himself did not want them recorded, or was it the writer's decision to omit them? It is because of this silence with regard to Ignatius' early life that the text begins in the year 1521, when Ignatius was thirty years old.

3. The Father's manner of narrating is the same he usually uses in everything else; he does it with such clarity that it seems that the whole past is made present to the listener. Thus, there was no need of my asking him any questions because whatever was essential to make the story intelligible the Father did not forget to relate. Without saying anything to the Father, I immediately went to write the points down, first sketchily and in my own hand, and later at greater length as it is now written. I have tried not to write a single word other than those that I have heard from the Father, and with regard to those where I fear I have failed it is because, not wanting to depart from the Father's words, I have not been able to properly explain the force of some of them. Thus, as I noted above, I was writing this up to September 1553, but from that time until Father Nadal arrived on October 18, 1554, the Father was continually giving excuses because of some illness or because various matters had to be attended to, telling me: "Remind me, when this business is over." And when it was over and I reminded him, he said: "Right now, we are busy with another matter. Remind me when this is finished."

4. When Father Nadal arrived he was very happy to see that the project was begun and told me to urge the Father to con-

---

4. By the time that Nadal had returned to Rome in October 1554, Ignatius' story had been interrupted for over a year, but he expressed his joy in hearing that at last the project he had requested was begun.[5] Then a whole series of affairs and events succeeded in prolonging the interruption. At one time it was the question of getting an endowment for the Roman College so that there would be no need to ask tuition of the students. Then it was the question of sending missionaries to Ethiopia. King John III of Portugal had been interested in bringing the Abyssinian Christians into the Catholic Church and had asked Ignatius to supply the missionaries. The belief, during the Middle Ages, was that the King of the Abyssinians was the legendary Prester John.

Ignatius resumed his narration on March 9, 1555, but it did not last long because Pope Julius III succumbed on the 23rd of that month and Ignatius postponed the project until a new pope had been elected. The new pontiff was Marcello Cervini, elected on April 9, who took the name of Marcellus II, but he died on May 1. He was then succeeded by Pope Paul

tinue, telling me many times that the Father could do nothing better for the Society than this, and that this was to give the Society's true foundations. He himself spoke to the Father many times, and the Father told me to jog his memory when the business of the college's endowment was completed. When that was over, then it was until the question of Prester John was settled and the courier had departed.

We began the story's continuation on March 9. Then Pope Julius III became critically ill and died on the 23rd, and the Father put the matter off until there was a new pope, but it happened that he too soon fell ill and died. This was Marcellus. The Father postponed everything until the election of Pope Paul IV. Afterwards, because of the heat and a great deal of business to attend to, he kept delaying until September 21, when the question arose about sending me to Spain. For this reason I strongly urged the Father to fulfill the promise he had made to me. So he made plans to meet me on the morning of the 22nd in the Red Tower. After I had said Mass I went to him to ask if this was the time.

5. He answered that I should go and wait for him in the Red Tower and that I should be there when he arrived. I took

---

IV (Gian Pietro Carafa), elected on May 23. The interruption continued throughout the summer and was resumed only because Gonçalves da Câmara had been told (September 21) that he would soon be going to Spain. Now that his days in Rome were numbered he pressed Ignatius to continue his story, and thus they arranged to meet on the 22nd in the Red Tower, a recently purchased building adjacent to the Society's residence.

5. Because of the writer's eagerness to read the expressions on Ignatius' face he seems to have approached too near so that Ignatius had asked him to observe the rule dealing with religious decorum that recommended that one should not stare fixedly on another's face, but that he should keep his eyes slightly lowered.[6] It is not known how many meetings there were before the writer's departure on October 23; in the Preface he indicates that the last meeting took place on October 22, but according to #99 of the text the final talk took place on the 20th. Because his departure was imminent the writer did not have the time to write down what he had received from Ignatius in any detail, but had to be satisfied with a few notes reflecting the gist of the narration. After the writer had arrived in Genoa,

it for granted that I would have to wait for him for some time, and so while I was in a hall talking to a brother, who had asked me a question, the Father came and reprimanded me for failing in obedience since I had not been waiting for him in the appointed place. That day he did not want to do anything. We then went to him and strongly urged him to continue. He returned to the Red Tower and dictated as he paced the floor, as he always did when dictating. I kept getting nearer and nearer to him so that I could better observe his facial expressions, but the Father said: "Observe the rule!" Forgetting this admonition, I again came near him, two or three times, and the Father repeated the admonition and went off. After some time he returned to the Tower to complete his dictation as we have it here written. Since I was, for some time, preparing to begin my journey (the eve of my departure was the last day that the Father had spoken to me on these matters), I was unable to write everything out in detail while in Rome. Not having a Spanish scribe in Genoa, I dictated in Italian, from the notes that I had brought with me from Rome, and I put the finishing touches to this narration in the month of December 1555, in Genoa.

and being unable to find a scribe capable of writing Spanish, he settled for an Italian, and thus he fleshed out his notes in poor Italian, and the scribe dutifully set them down. The general presumption is that the material received during the March 1555 meetings with Ignatius covered the Founder's life up to the beginning of #79 of the text and was written in Spanish, while the final portion, written in Italian, reflects the material of September-October.

According to the Preface, the writer completed the text of Ignatius' story in December 1555, while in Genoa. He may have written the Preface while in Genoa or while on his way to Portugal, but it does seem to have been written prior to Ignatius' death in 1556,[7] for he always refers to Ignatius in the present tense, and if Ignatius had already died one would have expected him to mention that fact in his Preface.[8]

Chapter 1
Pamplona–Loyola:
Convalescence and Conversion
(Mid-May 1521–Late February 1522)

1. Up to his twenty-sixth year he was a man given to worldly vanities, and having a vain and overpowering desire to gain renown, he found special delight in the exercise of arms. Thus he was in a fortress under attack by the French, and while everyone else clearly saw that they could not defend themselves and thought that they should surrender to save their lives, he

---

1. Ignatius twice mentions his age in this narration to Father Luis Gonçalves da Câmara. Here he says that he was twenty-six when injured at Pamplona, and since that occurred in 1521, it would mean that he was born in 1495. Later, in #30, Ignatius will state that in 1555 he was sixty-two years old, and that would then mean that he was born in 1493. This inconsistency has caused his biographers much anxiety. In the Introduction we have given 1491 as the probable date of Ignatius' birth, together with the reasons for choosing that date rather than 1493 or 1495. Ignatius was thus about thirty years old when he was wounded at Pamplona.

King Ferdinand the Catholic conquered the Kingdom of Navarre in 1512 and annexed it to Castile in 1515. To ensure Spanish control over Navarre, the walls of Pamplona, the capital, were strengthened and a new fortress overlooking the walls was constructed. Francis I of France likewise had his eyes on Navarre and in early 1521 moved to add it to his domain. French forces, under André de Foix, Lord of Asparros, made their way through southern France, crossed the Pyrenees, entered Navarre, and headed toward Pamplona. The Duke of Nájera, Vicerory of Navarre, left a garrison and artillery supplies in the fortress and some thousand men in the city while

7

offered so many reasons to the fortress' commander that he talked him into defending it. Though this was contrary to the opinion of all the other knights, still each drew encouragement from his firmness and fearlessness. When the day of the ex-

he, on May 17, went to Segovia to ask the Royal Council for reinforcements against the French. By the time the duke had arrived in Segovia, the French were but a few miles from Pamplona. The duke had previously sent word to Ignatius, who was then in Guipúzcoa, his native region, helping to quell a minor insurrection. In response to the duke's urgent request Ignatius enlisted the services of his elder brother, Martín García, together with men from the family's estate and from the province, and hastened to help keep the French from entering Pamplona.

Since there were many French sympathizers in Pamplona, these convinced the citizenry that it would be better to welcome the French than to have their city destroyed in a siege. When the two Loyola brothers and their forces arrived at the gates of Pamplona they joined Francés de Beaumont, leader of the Spanish garrison in the city, in trying to persuade the people to resist the French. They were unsuccessful, however, and seeing that the citizens were ready to capitulate to the French, Martín García turned his back on Pamplona and returned home. Ignatius remained, but when he learned that Francés de Beaumont likewise favored surrender, he took his men and rode to the citadel.

Since the city had decided to greet the French with open arms, Miguel de Herrera, commander of the fortress, felt that any defense on his part would be futile. The fortress would be attacked on all four sides and since his men were too few in number to withstand a prolonged siege, he too spoke of surrender. Ignatius, however, was of another opinion and he offered reasons why they should stand their ground and fight. These reasons have not been preserved, but undoubtedly one must have been that it would be shameful to surrender even before battle had begun. On May 19 Pamplona sent word to André de Foix that the city was his; he entered on the 20th and his men immediately set up their cannons and directed them against the fortress. These preparations were observed by Ignatius and the garrison and thus they expected the assault to begin that day. Since Ignatius intended to fight to his last breath, and because there was no chaplain among them, he asked one of his comrades to hear his confession of sin.[1] He was now prepared to meet death in the service of his king. The bombardment began that day and after six continuous hours of heavy shelling, a portion of the wall crumbled and a cannonball entered the fortress and shattered Ignatius' right leg.

pected assault came he made his confession to one of his comrades in arms and after the attack had lasted a good while, a cannonball hit him in a leg, shattering it completely, and since the ball passed between both legs the other one was likewise severely wounded.

2. As soon as he fell wounded the others in the fortress surrendered to the French who, after they had gained control, treated the wounded man very well, showing him courtesy and kindness. After being in Pamplona some twelve or fifteen days they transported him on a litter to his home country. His condition was serious and the physicians and surgeons, summoned from many places, agreed that the leg should be broken again and the bones reset, since they had been either poorly set in

2. With Ignatius now wounded, the other knights and artillery men began to lose courage and within days they surrendered the fortress to the French (May 23 or 24). Ignatius was taken into the city where French army surgeons set his leg and cared for his wounds. So kind were the French soldiers toward him that as a gesture of his appreciation Ignatius gave his shield to one of them, his dagger to another, and his cuirass to a third.[2] Today no trace of that fortress remains, but a church stands on the site dedicated to the one wounded there. Ignatius does not explicitly say who transported him to Loyola Castle; it could well have been some of the soldiers that he had brought with him from his family's estate, but it seems more likely that it was the French who had done so.[3] They carried the injured Ignatius on a litter and left Pamplona between June 2 and 5, and after passing through valleys and crossing mountains they made a stopover at Anzuola, where Ignatius' sister Magdalena resided.[4] The weary caravan arrived at Loyola between June 16 and 20.

Loyola Castle is situated between the towns of Azpeitia and Azcoitia, in the Basque province of Guipúzcoa, but when the wounded Ignatius returned in 1521, it was somewhat isolated from the towns and surrounded by woods. Since his father's death in 1507, and since Ignatius' eldest brother, Juan Pérez, had died in 1496, during the Spanish campaign against Naples, the Master of Loyola was his elder brother Martín García. Martín had married Magdalena de Araoz, one of Queen Isabella's ladies-in-waiting, in 1498, and brought her home to Loyola. At that time Ignatius was but a child of seven. Since Martín was then engaged in fighting the French at Logroño, it was Magdalena who welcomed Ignatius to the ancestral home and cared for him while the bone in his leg was reset.

the first place or had become dislocated during the journey, for they were now out of joint and would never heal. The butchery was repeated and during it, as in other such operations that he had undergone before and would later undergo, he never uttered a word nor did he show any sign of pain other than clenching his fists.

3. His condition grew much worse; he was unable to eat and, in addition, he had the usual signs indicating the approach of death. On Saint John's feast the physicians, not expecting him to pull through, advised him to make his confession. He received the sacraments and on the vigil of the feast of Saints Peter and Paul the physicians informed him that if he did not feel better by midnight he could count himself a dead man. Now, the sick man was devoted to Saint Peter, and our Lord thus desired that his recovery begin that very midnight. His improvement progressed so well that after a few days he was pronounced to be out of danger of death.

4. When the bones did knit together, the one below the knee rested on top of the other so that the leg was shortened and the bone so protruded that it made an unsightly bump. Because he was determined to make a way for himself in the

3. Ignatius was not home a week when his health so deteriorated that his physicians despaired of his life. On June 24, the feast of Saint John the Baptist, he received the last sacraments, but then at midnight, June 28, as the vigil of Saints Peter and Paul was ending and the feast beginning, Ignatius' health unexpectedly turned for the better. Saint John the Baptist and Saint Peter were two of Ignatius' patrons; the former was the patron of the Oñaz side of the family, and the latter was the patron of the Loyola side.[5] Both feasts were duly celebrated at the castle, and by noting that these events took place on the feasts of his patrons, Ignatius was indicating that he saw God's special intervention in his recovery.

4. Good news came to Loyola in early July. The French were finally defeated at Noaín on June 30, in which battle Martín García participated. All Navarre was again under Spanish control and the nation's flag was once more flying over the fortress in Pamplona. It was a happy Martín García that returned to find his brother recuperating on the castle's third floor, and as he narrated the events that led to the French defeat, perhaps Ignatius thought his wound was worth it.

world he could not tolerate such ugliness and thought it marred his appearance. Thus he instructed the surgeons to remove it, if possible. They told him that it could certainly be sawn away, but the pain would be greater than any he had suffered up to now, since the leg had healed and it would take some time to remove the bump. Nevertheless, he was determined to endure this martyrdom to satisfy his personal taste. His older brother was horrified and said that he himself would not dare undergo such pain, but the wounded man suffered it with his accustomed patience.

5. After the flesh and the excess bone had been cut away, they tried to keep the leg from being too short by applying many ointments and by using mechanical devices to keep it continually stretched. For many a day he had to endure this mar-

Ignatius still burned with the desire for worldly renown, but with one leg shorter than the other, and with an unsightly bone protruding, he knew he could never again wear the handsome close-fitting boots then in fashion. How could he dance? How could he project a dashing knightly appearance if he had a limp? There was but one answer — the offending bone would have to be cut away. While his brother recoiled at the thought of such an operation, Ignatius was determined to have it done so that he could continue his career in the world, and for that world he was willing to endure a martyrdom.

5. Ignatius not only submitted to this excruciating operation but he likewise submitted to a systematic stretching of his leg that meant weeks of pain and immobility.[6] By the end of August, or perhaps in early September, he felt sufficiently recovered to seek distraction and thus he asked his sister-in-law if there were in the castle any chivalrous romances, his favorite type of reading. Novels dealing with knightly exploits were the best-sellers of the sixteenth century. The most famous of these was *Amadís de Gaula*, which Ignatius acknowledged to have read (#17). A Castilian edition appeared in 1508, and was followed by a sequel and many imitations, many of them poor in quality. The titles of the other novels that Ignatius might have read are unknown to us, but he spent many an hour reading them while in Arévalo and while serving the Duke of Nájera.[7]

The Loyola household had none of these novels, so Magdalena offered him the only books she had. They were not exactly what Ignatius requested, but they would help him pass the time of day. She offered him the four volumes of *The Life of Jesus Christ* by Ludolph of Saxony (+ 1377), a Car-

tyrdom. But our Lord restored his health and he grew better. He was healthy in every respect except that he could not readily stand on that leg and he was thus forced to remain in bed. Since he was an avid reader of books of worldly fiction, commonly called chivalrous romances, and since he was feeling quite well, he asked for some such books to pass the time. In that house, however, they found none of the type he was used to reading and so they brought him *The Life of Christ* and a book on the lives of the saints in Spanish.

6. By frequent reading of these books he grew somewhat

thusian monk, and translated into Castilian by Ambrosio de Montesino, O.F.M., at the request of King Ferdinand and Queen Isabella, and which had been printed in Alcalá in 1502-1503. Ludolph's book was the first formal life of our Lord to appear in print and it was a wonderful blend of Scripture and the piety of the Middle Ages.[8] The other book that Magdalena gave him was the popular *Golden Legend* of Jacobo de Voragine, a Dominican, who died as Archbishop of Genoa in 1298. This book was more popularly known as *Flos sanctorum* because it contained brief lives of the saints. The translator of the Castilian version is anonymous, but it had been in circulation in Spain since 1480. The edition that Ignatius used was by the Cistercian Gauberto Maria Vagad, which first appeared in 1493 and was reprinted at Toledo in 1511. This was Ignatius' sole reading during his months of convalescence.

6. Ignatius read and reread passages from *The Life of Jesus Christ* and the lives of the saints in the *Flos sanctorum*. After a period of reading he usually paused to reflect on whatever touched him. While his reading found a definite response in his heart, he still found himself, at times, thinking that he was another Amadís performing heroic deeds for his lady. This lady of Ignatius' dreams has always remained elusive; since she was higher in station than a countess and a duchess, she then must have been a member of the royal family. Three have been suggested by Ignatius' various biographers.

(1) It has been proposed that the lady in question may have been Queen Germaine de Foix,[9] niece of Louis XII of France, and second wife of Ferdinand the Catholic. When Ferdinand died in 1516, Germaine was still in her early twenties. In 1519 she married the Margrave of Brandenburg and was still married to him at the time of Ignatius' daydreams. (2) Another candidate is the Infanta Catalina,[10] the youngest sister of Emperor Charles

fond of what he found written therein. Setting his reading aside, he sometimes paused to think about the things he had read, and at other times he thought of the worldly things that formerly occupied his mind. Of the many idle things that came to him, one took such a hold on his heart that, without his realizing it, it engrossed him for two or three hours at a time. He dreamed what he would achieve in the service of a certain lady and thought of the means he would take to go to the land where she lived, the clever sayings and words he would speak to her, and the knightly deeds he would perform for her. He was so enraptured with these thoughts of his that he never considered how impossible it was for him to accomplish them, for the lady was not one of the lesser nobility, neither was she a countess, nor a duchess, but her station was much higher than any of these.

7. Our Lord, nevertheless, came to his aid, bringing it about that these thoughts were followed by others arising from his reading. While reading the life of our Lord and those of the

V. She was born in 1507, but spent her entire youth in the gloomy surroundings of the royal palace at Tordesillas where her mother, the mad Queen Juana, was detained. When Charles convened the Cortes at Valladolid in February 1518, to receive the allegiance of the nobility, he brought Catalina to the city to present her to his court. She was only eleven, but contemporary accounts describe her as being most beautiful. Since Ignatius' new master, the Duke of Nájera, was present on that occasion, it is believed that Ignatius was likewise there and thus had his first glimpse of the royal princess. In 1524 Catalina married John III of Portugal, and after the Society of Jesus had been founded John III proved to be one of the best royal friends the Jesuits had ever known. (3) The final candidate is Leonor,[11] elder sister of Emperor Charles and Catalina, who was married to Manuel, King of Portugal, at the time of Ignatius' convalescence.

Was the lady of Ignatius' thoughts one of these three, or was she another? Ignatius chose to be silent on this point and it seems that her identity will always elude us.

7. The reading that Ignatius had done during his convalescence was, up to that time, the most important he had ever done, for it was through that reading that God began to act on his soul and draw him to a conver-

saints he used to pause and meditate, reasoning with himself: "What if I were to do what Saint Francis did, or to do what Saint Dominic did?" Thus in his thoughts he dwelt on many good deeds, always suggesting to himself great and difficult ones, but as soon as he considered doing them, they all appeared easy of performance. Throughout these thoughts he used to say to himself: "Saint Dominic did this, so I have to do it too. Saint Francis did this, so I have to do it too." These thoughts lasted a long time, but after other thoughts had taken their place, the above-mentioned worldly ones returned to him and he dwelt on them for quite some length. This succession of such diverse thoughts — of worldly exploits that he desired to accomplish, or those of God that came to his imagination — stayed with him for a long time as he turned them over in his mind, and when he grew weary of them he set them aside to think of other matters.

8. There was this difference, however. When he thought of worldly matters he found much delight, but after growing weary and dismissing them he found that he was dry and un-

---

sion of life. Ignatius was familiar with the Dominican and Franciscan Orders, for they were not only the two most popular Orders in the sixteenth century, but each had convents in the various cities and towns of Spain. There even was a Franciscan convent in Azpeitia, one of whose foundresses was his relative Maria López de Emparán y Loyola.[12] It is not surprising then that Ignatius should want to dwell on the lives of Saints Dominic and Francis, but what is noteworthy is that he did not merely conclude that their lives were imitable, but that he saw himself obliged to imitate them — that he too had to accomplish for God what they had accomplished.

8-9. Because of the various movements that Ignatius experienced in his soul during his months of convalescence, he eventually learned how to discern the spirits moving him. He came to realize that thoughts about the world left him dry and unhappy, while thoughts of a pilgrimage to Jerusalem and penance brought him happiness and joy. He concluded that the former came from the devil while the latter came from God. Chief among the thoughts that produced joy was the idea of going to Jerusalem and this desire most surely had its origin in his reading of Ludolph's life of Christ. The Prooemium to that book, written by a Dominican of the thirteenth century,

happy. But when he thought of going barefoot to Jerusalem and of eating nothing but vegetables and of imitating the saints in all the austerities they performed, he not only found consolation in these thoughts but even after they had left him he remained happy and joyful. He did not consider nor did he stop to examine this difference until one day his eyes were partially opened and he began to wonder at this difference and to reflect upon it. From experience he knew that some thoughts left him sad while others made him happy, and little by little he came to perceive the different spirits that were moving him; one coming from the devil, the other coming from God.

9. He gained not a little light from this lesson and he began to think more seriously about his past life and how greatly he needed to do penance for it. It was at this time that the desire to imitate the saints came to him, and without giving any consideration to his present circumstances, he promised to do, with God's grace, what they had done. His greatest desire, after regaining his health, was to go to Jerusalem, as previously stated, and to observe the fasts and to practice the discipline as any generous soul on fire with God is accustomed to do.

10. With these holy desires of his, the thoughts of his former life were soon forgotten and this was confirmed by a vision

and appropriated by Ludolph to serve as his introduction, tells the reader of the delight that fills the heart when visiting the Holy Land. What joy to see the places where our Lord visited and to reflect that it was in those very places that our Lord worked our salvation! Ignatius' vivid imagination soon transported him to Jerusalem, and once that desire had taken hold of his heart he would not rest until it had been fulfilled. In addition, he intended to keep to a strict vegetarian diet and to practice the austerities practiced by the saints whose lives he had read in the *Flos sanctorum*.

10. Now that Ignatius set aside the worldly thoughts that had once attracted him and decided to follow Christ after the example of His saints, his decision received divine confirmation. Ignatius simply relates that one evening, unable to fall asleep, he saw "the likeness of our Lady with the holy Child Jesus." He does not indicate whether he had seen her with his bodily eyes, or whether it was with the eyes of his mind, that is, an in-

in this manner. One night, as he lay sleepless, he clearly saw
the likeness of our Lady with the holy Child Jesus, and because
of this vision he enjoyed an excess of consolation for a remarkably
long time. He felt so great a loathsomeness for all his past life,
especially for the deeds of the flesh, that it seemed to him that
all the images that had been previously imprinted on his mind
were now erased. Thus from that hour until August 1553, when
this is being written, he never again consented, not even in
the least matter, to the motions of the flesh. Because of this
effect in him he concluded that this had been God's doing,
though he did not dare to specify it any further, nor say anything
more than to affirm what he had said above. His brother interpreted his external change, as did other members of the
household, to mean that an interior change had taken place in
his soul.

11. Free of all cares, he continued his reading and his good
resolves. During the time he spent talking to the members of
the household he spoke about the things of God and he thus

terior experience. Nor does he indicate if our Lady had spoken to him. What
is clear is that he experienced her presence and that it had the remarkable
result that from that moment onward he was filled with a total disgust
for his former way of life. Through this signal grace Ignatius saw himself
as one transformed; his former self now yielded to the true follower of Christ.
Ignatius never revealed the date when this wondrous grace had come to
him; August 15, 1521, has been suggested,[13] but it could well have been
later, perhaps in September. This change in Ignatius did not go unnoticed.
His brother observed that he was no longer the soldier he once had been,
and his conversation was no longer about wars and knights but of God
and His saints. Ignatius' conversion to God was now in progress and the
power of that vision remained with him to the end of his life.

11. God was now the focal point of Ignatius' life, and his entire day
was spent in prayer, reading, and writing. Because he wanted to preserve
some of the thoughts he found in his books, he decided to jot them down
for future use. He took an account book—it was quarto in size and had
300 pages—and in it wrote our Lord's words in red ink, just as he had
seen them in Ludolph's life of Christ, but it was his own idea to record
those of our Lady in blue. This book, unfortunately, must have been lost

brought much profit to their souls. He greatly enjoyed his books and the idea struck him to copy down, in abridged form, the more important items in the life of Christ and of the saints. Now that he began to get out of bed and move around the house a little, he set about writing these things in a book, taking great care and using red ink for Christ's words and blue for those of our Lady. He used polished and lined paper and wrote in a good hand since he had an attractive penmanship. He spent some of his time in writing and some in prayer. The greatest consolation he received at this time was from gazing at the sky and stars, and this he often did and for quite a long time. The result of all this was that he felt within himself a strong impulse to serve our Lord. He spent much time reflecting on his resolution and wished to be fully recovered so that he could set out on his journey.

12. Mulling over his plans and thinking of what he would do after he had returned from Jerusalem so that he could live a

at an early date as none of Ignatius' first companions appears to have seen it. All they knew about it was its size and how many pages it had.[14] Now being able to move about the house and grounds, Ignatius took to gazing at the stars, a practice that stayed with him. Off the rooms he occupied in Rome as Father General there is a small balcony and there of an evening Ignatius frequently stood to look upon the Roman sky. As his health steadily improved, so grew his eagerness to begin his pilgrimage.

12. Ignatius was determined to go to the Holy Land, but what would he do when he returned home? His first thought was to enter the famous monastery of Nuestra Señora de las Cuevas on the outskirts of Seville. His choice of the Carthusians may have come from the fact that Ludolph was a Carthusian, as well as their reputation for being the most penitential of Orders in the Church. Among the Carthusians he would be able to live a life of penance as he desired and observe their rule of doing without meat. Because Seville was in southern Spain Ignatius felt that no one would know him there, nor would any one have heard of him, and thus in complete anonymity he could give himself to God.[15] But then a doubt came to mind: perhaps the rules of the Order would not permit him to live as severe a life as he would like? In that case he thought of living in the world, but following a life of penance.

life of constant penance, he thought of entering the Carthusian monastery in Seville, where he would not reveal his identity — so that they would not think much of him — and where his diet would be only vegetables. But when he again thought of the penances he wanted to fulfill as he went about the world, his desire for the Carthusian way of life cooled since he feared that there he would not be able to give vent to the hatred that he had conceived against himself. Nevertheless, when a house servant was going to Burgos he asked him to gather information about the Carthusian rule, and the information he received seemed satisfactory.

Ignatius had not totally given up on the Carthusians for when he learned that one of his brother's servants was going to Burgos, some sixty miles south of Loyola, he asked him to get some information about the Carthusian rule. The monastery was known as La Real Cartuja de Miraflores. This was originally a royal hunting lodge, but in 1442 it was offered to the Carthusians, who still maintain it as a monastery. When Ignatius was enjoying *Amadís de Gaula* he read that it was to Miraflores that King Lisuarte and his wife retired after they had abdicated the English throne in favor of Amadís and his wife Oriana.

In Ignatius' plans Jerusalem came before the monastery, and now that he felt strong enough to travel he did not want to postpone his departure any longer. Knowing how his brother would react if he had been told his plans in full, Ignatius merely informed him that it was time for him to visit the Duke of Nájera, who was then at Navarrete. Martín García sensed that Ignatius was not just going to visit the duke, and so before he departed, both brothers took a stroll through the family castle, visiting room after room. They recalled all who had lived there, their parents as well as their brothers who had died in battle. They spoke of the important events in their family's history and its proud heritage in the service of the kings of Castile. Martín García endeavored to show Ignatius that he had a bright military career before him and that the Loyola name was greatly honored and respected in northern Spain. Still, the brother's persuasion did not have its hoped-for result for Ignatius was as determined as ever to dedicate himself to God. To be a knight in the service of an earthly king was now something in his past; Ignatius looked forward to being a knight in the service of an eternal King. It was late February 1522.

Because of the above-mentioned reason and because his mind was fully taken up with the journey that he was thinking of soon making, and since entering the monastery was something that could wait until his return, he did not think much more about it. Feeling that his strength had sufficiently returned, he judged it was time to depart and he told his brother: "My Lord, the Duke of Nájera, as you are aware, knows that I am again well. It will be good for me to get to Navarrete." (The duke was residing there at the time.) His brother led him from room to room and with much love for him pleaded with him not to throw his life away, but to acknowledge the great hopes people had placed in him, and to see what he could make of himself. These and other similar arguments were all directed to dissuade him from his good desire, but without departing from the truth, for he was now very scrupulous about that, he answered in a way that enabled him to leave his brother.

Chapter 2

Montserrat: A Knight's Vigil
(Late February — March 25, 1522)

13. As he mounted his mule, another brother of his wanted to travel with him as far as Oñate, and on the way he persuaded him to keep a vigil at the shrine of Our Lady of Aránzazu.

13. Hearing that Ignatius was about to leave for Navarrete, Pero López, Ignatius' priest-brother, asked to travel with him as far as Oñate, where he intended to visit their sister. Pero López had been Ignatius' companion in the carnival excesses in 1515, for which both had been brought before the magistrate in Guipúzcoa. Since 1518 Pero López was pastor of the church of San Sebastián de Soreasu in Azpeitia. Dressed as befitted his noble rank, with sword at his side, and accompanied by two attendants, Ignatius and his brother left Loyola Castle and headed southward. Ignatius planned on visiting the shrine of Our Lady of Aránzazu, so he talked his brother into first making a night vigil with him at the shrine and then proceeding to Oñate. The shrine, at the time of Ignatius' visit, was only fifty years old and had been built on the site where a Basque shepherd boy found a statue of our Lady nestled in a thorny bush. During his vigil Ignatius placed his journey to Jerusalem under our Lady's care and asked heaven for the health and strength needed to fulfill his pilgrimage. It was most probably at Aránzazu that Ignatius made a vow of chastity. In later years he acknowledged that he had made the vow during his journey from Loyola to Montserrat, but since he did not divulge the name of the place where he had made it, his biographers think that the shrine of Aránzazu would have been a suitable place for such a vow.

After a night of prayer the brothers and servants headed northwest to Oñate where Ignatius left Pero López with their sister. It is unclear which sister was then in Oñate, but it is presumed that it was Magdalena, recently married in Anzuola to Juan López de Gallaiztegui, and who was now visiting

That night he prayed for additional strength for his journey. He then left his brother in Oñate at the home of a sister of theirs, whom his brother was going to visit, and went on toward Navarrete. Remembering that the duke's household owned him some ducats, he thought it a good time to collect them and so he penned a note to the treasurer who responded that he was short of funds, but when the duke heard this he said that he could owe money to everyone else, but he must pay his debts to Loyola. The duke wanted to offer him — in recognition for what he had accomplished in the past — a position of authority, if he would accept it. He collected his money and ordered that it be divided among certain individuals to whom he felt some obligation, and that a part of it be used for a statue of our Lady that was poorly appointed and which he wanted to be more appropriately decorated and ornamented. Saying good-bye to the two servants who traveled with him, he departed Navarrete and, riding his mule, he headed for Montserrat.

14. Something happened as he was on his way and it will be good to record it so that others may understand how our

the Araoz family.[1] Taking leave of his brother and sister, Ignatius directed his mule toward Navarrete, near Logroño. Since the duke was then visiting Nájera, Ignatius submitted his bill, for services rendered in 1521, to the duke's treasurer, and since the duke had recently lost favor with his sovereign and had been replaced as viceroy in Navarre, the treasury may have been somewhat strained. Hearing that Ignatius was in Navarrete, the duke sent word that he was to be paid what was owed him and, in addition, he offered him an important position, but Ignatius declined it. He spent part of the money he received settling unpaid debts and the remainder was to be used to refurbish an image of our Lady, perhaps in the church of Navarrete itself, or at a nearby shrine.[2] Having settled his accounts, Ignatius sent his servants back to Loyola and made his way alone toward Montserrat.

14. Looking back, after some thirty years, on himself and on the way he had first expressed his fervor, Ignatius acknowledged that he was at that time still blind and uneducated in the spiritual life. To be sure, he desired to follow Christ, and to do this he chose to imitate the saints he had met

Lord dealt with that soul, still blind but filled with ardent
desires to follow Him in every way he knew. Thus he decided
to practice great penances, not with the view of satisfying for
his sins but to please and appease God. Whenever he made up
his mind to do a certain penance that the saints had done, he
was determined not only to do the same, but even more. All
his consolation derived from these thoughts; he never considered
anything about the interior life, nor did he know what humility
was or charity, or patience, or that discretion was the rule and
measure of these virtues. His only intention, not having any
other reason in mind, was to perform these important external
actions because the saints had performed them for the glory
of God.

15. As he continued his way a Moor riding on a mule caught
up with him, and in their conversation they began to speak

in his reading during his months of convalescence. Whatever penances they
had practiced, those he would also perform. The saints had likewise sub-
jected their bodies to the discipline, even to the drawing of blood, and he
would do the same. Now that he had left his home behind and was alone
on his journey, he began taking the discipline, but he saw this more as
a sign of his love for God than as satisfaction for sins. As for the need to
grow in virtue, of this Ignatius was still ignorant, and his mention of discretion perhaps indicates that he thought his former penances should have been
regulated by it.

15-16. On leaving Navarrete, Ignatius, who now refers to himself simply
as "the pilgrim," went to Logroño and there met the royal highway leading
to Saragossa, the capital of Aragón. He passed through Calahorra and Tudela
and as he was approaching Pedrola, a town some twenty-three miles west
of Saragossa, he had his strange encounter with a Moor. As Ignatius was
making his way on the road a Moor caught up with him and fell into conversation with him. Since the conversation focused on our Lady it is not
difficult to surmise that Ignatius must have told him that he was on his
way to Montserrat to visit our Lady's shrine. Because the Muslims are faithful
readers of the Koran they hold Mary, the mother of Jesus, in esteem.
Together with Christians they maintain that our Lord was miraculously
conceived in Mary's womb, for the Koran states: "She said: 'O my Lord!
How shall I have a son when no man has touched me?' "[3] But the Muslims

about our Lady. The Moor said that it certainly seemed to him that the Virgin had conceived without the aid of man, but he could not believe that in giving birth she remained a virgin. To substantiate his opinion, he offered the natural reasons that occurred to him. Though the pilgrim countered with many arguments he could not alter the Moor's opinion. The Moor then went on ahead in great haste so that he lost sight of him; being left behind, he reflected on what took place between him and the Moor. Various emotions welled up in him and he became disturbed in soul, thinking that he had failed to do what he should have done. Filled with anger against the Moor and thinking that he had done wrong in allowing a Moor to utter such things about our Lady, he concluded that he was obliged

separate themselves from Christians when they teach that Jesus' birth was natural and that it took place beneath a tree. On this point the Koran reads: "So she conceived him, and she retired with him to a remote place. And the pains of childbirth drove her to the trunk of a palm tree and she cried in anguish."[4]

Hearing the Moor's position on our Lady's perpetual virginity, Ignatius entered into discussion with him and brought forward as many arguments as he could to prove that Mary was not only a virgin before Jesus' birth, but also during and after it. Feeling that the discussion was becoming somewhat heated and seeing that Ignatius had a sword at his side, the Moor abruptly spurred his donkey onward and left Ignatius far behind. The code of chivalry, with which Ignatius was brought up and according to whose tenets he had lived his life, told him that he had done grievous wrong in permitting an infidel to insult our Lady. The Moor's remarks had to be punished and our Lady's honor restored! Thus the Amadís in Ignatius urged him to use his dagger on the Moor, but the Ignatius who fell in love with the saints knew that those who take up the sword would die by the sword. Thus, he was torn apart by an internal conflict, and unable to decide what to do he determined to leave the matter in God's hands. As the mule was coming to a fork in the road that led to Pedrola,[5] where the Moor had gone, he gently placed the reins in his lap and waited to see which road the mule would take. Would it continue on the highway, or would it go down to Pedrola? Since the mule chose to remain on the highway, Ignatius interpreted this as God's will.

to restore her honor. He now desired to search out the Moor and strike him with his dagger for all that he had said. This conflict in his desires remained with him for some time, but in the end he was still uncertain for he did not know what was required of him. The Moor, who had gone on ahead, had told him that he was going to a place a little farther on the same route, near the royal highway but that the highway did not pass through the place.

16. Tired of trying to figure out what would be the good thing to do, and unable to come to any definite decision, he determined on the following, namely, to give the mule free rein and to let it go by itself to the point where the roads met. If the mule took the road to the village, he would then search out the Moor and use his dagger on him; if the mule took the highway and not the village road, he would then let the Moor go scot-free. And he did just as he decided. Our Lord brought it about that though the village was little more than thirty or forty paces away and the road leading to it was quite wide and in good condition, the mule chose the highway and disregarded the village road.

Coming to a large town before reaching Montserrat, he there wanted to purchase the clothes he intended to wear when he

---

After the meeting with the Moor Ignatius passed through Saragossa — without stopping, for he tried to avoid crowds — and after traversing some 150 more miles he came to Igualada, a town situated at the foot of Montserrat. Before ascending the craggy mountain he thought it time to purchase the few items he would need for his journey to Jerusalem. Igualada[6] was known for its cloth-making, and there Ignatius bought some rough burlap-type cloth that the local people used for making sacks, and had a long tunic made for himself. In addition he purchased a gourd for water, a staff to aid his walking, and sandals for his wounded foot. Once he had placed everything in his saddlebag he turned his mule toward the road that pilgrims used to reach the shrine on top of the "serrated mountain." After some twenty days of travel, and after covering some 350 miles,[7] Ignatius was now ready to present himself before our Lady.

went to Jerusalem. He bought some sackcloth—it was of a loose weave and bristly to the touch—and asked them to make it into a long garment that would go down to his feet. he bought himself a pilgrim's staff and a small hollow gourd, and attached everything to the saddle atop his mule.

17. He continued his way to Montserrat thinking, as he usually did, of the achievements he was going to perform for

---

17. It was March 21, 1522, when Ignatius climbed the road to the shrine. His thoughts were filled with what he was about to do. The feast of the Annunciation was approaching; he would make his confession, divest himself of his rich robes and invest himself in pilgrim's garb, and then make his vigil before our Lady's statue. From his reading of the fourth book of *Amadís de Gaula* Ignatius recalled how Amadís' son, Esplandián, on the occasion of his consecration as a knight, made his vigil of arms before a statue of the Blessed Virgin. Ignatius was determined to do the same.

Arrived at the shrine Ignatius stabled his mule, registered at the pilgrims' hostel, and went to pray before our Lady's image. The abbey was celebrated throughout Europe for its reform movement, but it was because of the dark brown, almost black, statue, which the faithful considered miraculous, that countless pilgrims came to pray in the shrine church. On his first day Ignatius met the priest assigned to hear the confessions of the pilgrims, Dom Jean Chanon, a Frenchman, who had come to the abbey in 1512. Ignatius made known his desire to made a general confession of his life and to help prepare for it Dom Jean gave him a copy of the *Exercitatory of the Spiritual Life*, a manual prepared by an abbot of Montserrat, García Jiménez de Cisneros, and printed at the abbey in 1500.[8] For the next three days Ignatius fasted on bread and water as he followed the meditations in Cisneros' book and began examining his conscience, writing down his life's sins as best he remembered them. Then, on the eve of the Annunciation, he read his list to his confessor and received absolution.

Though Ignatius had been thinking of making a pilgrimage to Jerusalem for some seven months, he had never revealed these plans to anyone. At Montserrat he told them to Dom Jean; he narrated how God had been working in his soul, how he desired to renounce the world and go to Jerusalem and spend his life doing penance for the love of God. Before he took leave of his confessor Ignatius told him that he was leaving his mule to the monastery and asked that his dagger and sword be placed with the other ex-votos on the walls or grille of our Lady's chapel.

the love of God. As his thoughts were fully occupied with exploits, such as he read in *Amadís de Gaula* and other like books,
similar thoughts also came to mind. He therefore determined
to keep a night's vigil over his arms; he would neither sit nor
lie down, but would stand and kneel before the altar of Our
Lady of Montserrat, where he had decided to set aside the
garments he was wearing and clothe himself in the livery of
Christ. Having left that place he continued, as usual, thinking
of his projected plans, and when he arrived at Montserrat, he
offered a prayer and arranged for a confessor. He made a general
confession in writing, which lasted three days, and arranged
with his confessor to leave his mule behind and to hang his
sword and dagger at our Lady's altar in the church. The confessor was the first man to whom he revealed his plans, for
up to now he had never told them to any confessor.

18. On the eve of our Lady's feast in March, in the year
1522, he went at night, as secretly as he could, to a poor man
and, removing all his clothing, he gave it to the poor man and
dressed himself in the garment he so desired to wear, and went
to kneel before our Lady's altar. He spent the entire night there,
sometimes on his knees, sometimes standing erect, with his

18. As evening came on, March 24, the last things he had to give away
were the very clothes he was wearing, and finding a beggar at the shrine,
he gave him his robes and donned his pilgrim's tunic. With only a staff
in hand he went to the church and chose a place before the grille that
separated our Lady's chapel from the body of the church. Other pilgrims
were also there, in prayer, preparing themselves for our Lady's great feast.
Ignatius stood among them unnoticed. Throughout the night, now kneeling, now standing, according to the code of chivalry, Ignatius watched
in our Lady's presence, asking her to take him under her protection. Just
before day was about to break, monks filed into the chapel and began singing anthems in honor of the Blessed Virgin. Ignatius then participated in
the Mass that followed and received Holy Communion. When the Mass
was over he immediately left to be on his way. His hasty departure from
the shrine can be accounted for by his desire not to be recognized as the
noble who had come in robes but was now leaving in sackcloth.

pilgrim's staff in hand. At break of day he departed so as not to be recognized, and he took not the main road that led directly to Barcelona, on which road he could meet many who knew and respected him, but a detour to a town called Manresa, where he decided he would remain for several days in a hospital and jot down a few items in the book which he guardedly carried with him and which afforded him much consolation.

After he had traveled about a league from Montserrat, a man who had been pursuing him caught up with him and asked if he had given some clothing to a certain poor man as the poor man claimed. As he answered that he had done so, tears of compassion rolled from his eyes in behalf of the man to whom he had given his clothes — tears of compassion because he realized that the man was now being suspected of having stolen them. For as much as he fled the esteem of others, he was not long in Manresa before people were saying great things about him, all because of what had happened at Montserrat. His reputation grew and the people were saying more than what was true: that he had renounced a huge inheritance and other such things.

Rather than going directly to Barcelona to get passage for Italy and the Holy Land, Ignatius thought of going to some out-of-the-way place where he could spend a few days continuing his reflections and have the time to write down in his book the thoughts that had come to him while at Montserrat. Thus he avoided the royal highway and took a side road that eventually took him to Manresa. Not long after he had left the shrine, an individual who had been running after him caught up with him and asked whether he had given his clothing to a beggar, for the beggar was now suspected of being a thief. Ignatius readily admitted that his clothes were a gift to the man, but realizing that his good deed had caused the poor man some inconvenience, his eyes filled with tears of compassion. Having settled that affair, Ignatius set his steps toward Manresa, not knowing what was before him.

Chapter 3

Manresa: Taught by God
(March 25, 1522–Mid-March 1523)

19. While in Manresa he begged alms every day. He ate no meat, nor did he drink wine, though both were offered him. On Sundays he did not fast, and if someone gave him wine, he drank it. And because he had been quite meticulous in caring for his hair, which was according to the fashion of the day — and he had a good crop of hair — he decided to let it grow naturally without combing, cutting, or covering it with anything

19. On March 25, 1522, Ignatius saw the town of Manresa before him. He crossed the bridge over the Cardoner river and asked for lodging at a hospital for the poor named after Saint Lucy and located outside the town's walls. In exchange for his bed the pilgrim helped about the hospital; his food he begged in the city. He originally planned to spend but a few days there and then go to Barcelona so that he could be in Italy by late spring to meet the pilgrim ship going to Jerusalem. But the few days turned into ten months. Ignatius does not tell us what changed his mind. Was it the plague in the spring of 1522 that prevented him from going to Barcelona, or did he feel that he must better prepare himself by greater penance? Whatever the reason, Ignatius remained in Manresa and imitated the eccentric Egyptian hermit, Saint Onuphrius or Humphrey, who, as he read in the *Flos sanctorum*, let his hair grow until his entire body had been covered. Intent on imitating the saints and on gaining a complete victory over himself, Ignatius likewise let his hair grow long and wild, and no longer cared for the nails on his hands and feet.

Ignatius' early days in Manresa were days of peace and spiritual joy. He found a cave where he went to pray and do penance; he was accustomed to spend seven hours a day in prayer, take the discipline three times a day, work in the hospital, beg his daily food, and attend services in the local

either during the day or night. For the same reason he let the
nails of his feet and hands grow since he had also been overly
neat with regard to them. While living in this hospital it many
times happened that in full daylight he saw a form in the air
near him and this form gave him much consolation because it
was exceedingly beautiful. He did not understand what it really
was, but it somehow seemed to have the shape of a serpent
and had many things that shone like eyes, but were not eyes.
He received much delight and consolation from gazing upon
this object and the more he looked upon it, the more his consolation increased, but when the object vanished he became
disconsolate.

20. Up to this time he continued undisturbed in the same
interior state of great and constant joy without knowing
anything about internal spiritual matters. During the days that
the vision lasted, or a little before it began— for it endured
many days—a disturbing thought came to torment him, point-

---

church. It was at Manresa that he saw—and not once or twice but sometimes
six or seven times a day—that strange serpentine form with its seven or
eight shining eyes that were not really eyes.[1] At first Ignatius did not know
what this form was nor what it meant, but sometime later, as he explains
in #31, he came to know that it was the devil, and though he recognized
it for what it was, that form, nevertheless, continued to appear for the
next fifteen years, that is, until Ignatius went to Rome.

20. During his days of consolation Ignatius was faced with this temptation: the manner of life that he had chosen was impossible to live; he
could do it for a time, to be sure, but he could never persevere until death.
Since he had already made his decision to follow Christ and now refused
to go back on his word, the temptation vanished. He notes that the temptation occurred at the time he was entering the church where he usually
went to attend Mass and participate in the divine office. This church was
probably the collegiate church called the Seo, since Manresa had once been
an episcopal see. With him he had a *Book of Hours*, a prayer book containing the psalms and prayers for the different parts of the office, and during
Ignatius' time these books usually included the Passion narrative from Saint
John's Gospel, or a harmonized version of the Passion based on the four
evangelists.[2]

ing out to him the burdensomeness of his life. It was like someone speaking within his soul: "And how will you be able to
put up with this for the seventy years you have ahead of you?"
Perceiving that this was the voice of the enemy, he likewise
interiorly answered and with great courage: "O, you wretch!
Can you promise me one hour of life?" Thus he overcame the
temptation and remained tranquil. This was the first temptation he experienced after the above incident and it happened
as he was going into the church where he daily attended High
Mass as well as Vespers and Compline, which were always sung,
and from which he derived great consolation. He usually read
the Passion at Mass, always maintaining his soul in serene peace.

21. After the above-mentioned temptation, he began to feel
notable changes in his soul. Sometimes he was so dejected that
he found no enjoyment in the prayers he recited, not even in
attending Mass, nor in any other form of prayer. Sometimes

21. Ignatius now enters the second stage of his spiritual development,
a period of darkness of soul. His attendance at Mass sometimes produced
consolation in him, but at other times it brought about arid desolation.
Because he was still a novice in the way of the spiritual life, he was unable
to decipher what was happening within him, but he recognized that
something profound was taking place in his soul and this made him wonder:
"What kind of a new life is this that we are now beginning?" Considered
by some in Manresa as a spiritual person — though Ignatius claimed that
he had no knowledge of spiritual matters — individuals sought his advice,
seeking to learn how they could better serve God. He does not tell us who
these individuals were, but among those with whom he spoke, one especially
impressed him, and that was an elderly woman who was sufficiently famous
for King Ferdinand to request to see her. This woman still remains unknown
despite the efforts of Ignatius' biographers to identify her. Then almost as
an afterthought he mentions his custom of going to confession and receiving Holy Communion each week. This custom was probably recommended
to him by his confessor, Dom Jean Chanon, at Montserrat, and he, in turn,
recommended it to all who sought his advice. Weekly Communion was
uncommon in the sixteenth century and the Church had to wait until the
time of Pope Saint Pius X, in the early part of the twentieth century, to
change its custom.

the exact opposite happened to him, and so suddenly that it seemed he had stripped away all sadness and desolation, just as one strips a cloak from another's shoulders. He was astonished at these changes, which he had never before experienced, and said to himself: "What kind of a new life is this that we are now beginning?" At this time he sometimes spoke with spiritual persons who respected him and desired to converse with him, and though he had no knowledge of spiritual matters, nevertheless his words manifested a great fervor and a firm will to advance in God's service.

There was in Manresa, at the time, a woman advanced in years, who had been for a long time a servant of God and was known as such in many parts of Spain, so much so that the Catholic King had once summoned her to seek her advice. One day this woman, chatting with Christ's new soldier, said to him: "May it please my Lord Jesus Christ to appear to you some day!" He was quite surprised at her remark, and understanding the words in a literal way, asked: "How would Jesus Christ appear to me?" Every Sunday he continued his usual custom of confessing his sins and receiving Communion.

22. Now he began to be greatly troubled with scruples. Though he had made a general confession at Montserrat and

22-24. Some time after his coming to Manresa, Ignatius was severely tormented by scruples. He felt that he had not confessed certain sins as he should have, and though he confessed them again and again his soul was still without peace. He sought help from various priests but none was able to help him. He notes that he went to confession to the priest who regularly preached at the cathedral,[3] and following his advice, made another general confession as he had done at Montserrat, but still without peace. By this time he had left his room at the hospital and was living in a cell on the ground floor of the Dominican monastery, which the monks had kindly offered him. He took his problem to his Dominican confessor,[4] but his burden remained with him. Ignatius nevertheless continued his prayers and penances, and at midnight rose to attend Matins in the Dominican church. Having suffered his scruples for several months, Ignatius was prepared to try any remedy, no matter how difficult or how ridiculous,

had done so with great care, having written everything out, as it was said, at times it still seemed to him that he had not confessed certain things. This brought him much suffering for even though he had confessed everything he was still not satisfied. Thus he began to look about for some spiritual men who would cure him of his scruples, but nothing helped him. Finally, a learned man connected with the cathedral chapter, who was a very spiritual man and who used to preach there, one day told him in confession to write down all that he could remember. This he did, but even after he had confessed all this, his scruples returned even with regard to small and piddling matters, so that he was deeply distressed. Though he understood that these scruples were doing him much harm and it would be good to be free of them, still he could not cast them off. He sometimes thought that his cure would lie in his confessor ordering him in the name of Jesus Christ not to confess anything more from his past life, and he desired his confessor to so order him, but he did not dare suggest this to him.

23. Without having to ask, his confessor ordered him not to confess anything more from his past unless it was something abundantly clear. But since he considered everything manifestly clear, the order benefited him not at all, and thus he continued in his anxiety. At this time he was living in a small room that the Dominicans had given him in their monastery, and there he kept to his custom of praying seven hours a day on his knees, of rising every midnight, and of performing all the other exercises previously mentioned. In all this he found no cure for his scruples; they had now been tormenting him for several months. Once, being very disturbed because of them, he set himself to pray and with great fervor he cried aloud to God, saying: "Help

if only he could find relief. So debilitating was this torment that he even contemplated suicide,[5] but then he remembered what Saint Andrew,[6] whom he encountered in his reading, had once done. In imitation of him Ignatius decided neither to eat nor drink anything until God had freed him of his scruples.

me, Lord, for I find no remedy among men, nor in any creature. No task would be too irksome for me if I thought I could get help. Lord, show me where I may get it, and even if I have to follow after a little puppy to get the remedy I need, I will do it."

24. Taken up with these thoughts he was many times vehemently tempted to throw himself into a deep hole in his room which was near the place where he used to pray. But realizing that it was a sin to kill oneself, he again cried out: "Lord, I will do nothing to offend You." He many times repeated these words as well as the former ones. He remembered the story of a saint who, in order to obtain from God something he very much desired, went without eating for many days until he received it. Spending much time thinking of this idea he finally decided to do the same, telling himself that he would neither eat nor drink until God had granted his request, or until he saw that death was near. For if he saw himself *in extremis* and was about to die because of not eating, he decided that he would then ask for bread and eat it (for in such extreme circumstances he would be permitted to ask for it and eat it).

25. One Sunday, after he had received Communion, he started his fast. He went through an entire week without putting anything in his mouth, but at the same time he continued his usual exercises, participating in the divine office, praying on his knees, rising at midnight, and so forth. When the following Sunday came, it was again time for him to go to confession, and since he was in the habit of telling his confessor everything he did with all its details, he also told him how

25. By obeying his confessor with regard to giving up his fast, Ignatius' scruples left him for a time, but then they returned, and with them the temptation to abandon his new way of life. It was this temptation that awakened him, as if from a deep sleep, for he now understood whence those scruples had come, and his decision never again to confess his past sins brought him the freedom he sought for so long a time. Ignatius does not attribute this freedom to anything that he himself may have done, but views it as a gift of God's mercy.

he had eaten nothing that week. The confessor ordered him
to break off his fast and though he was still feeling strong, he
nevertheless obeyed his confessor, and that day as well as the
following day he found that he was free of his scruples. But
on the third day, which was a Tuesday, the remembrance of
his sins returned to him while he was at prayer, and as one
thing leads to another, he thought of sin after sin from his past
life and felt obliged to confess them again. After these thoughts,
there came upon him a loathing for the life he was then living
and he had a strong temptation to give it up. In this manner
the Lord chose to awaken him as from a dream. Now that he
had some experience with the different spirits—through the
lessons that God had given him—he began to think about the
way that that spirit had come to him. Thus he decided, and
with great clarity of mind, never to confess his past sins again
and from that day forward he was free of his scruples, and he
held it for certain that our Lord had desired to set him free
because of His mercy.

26. In addition to his seven hours of prayer, he spent time
in helping other souls who came there to see him about spiritual
matters, and the rest of the day he gave to thinking about the
things of God that he had read or meditated on that day. But
often when he went to bed, great spiritual lights came to him,

---

26. Among the books Ignatius had at Manresa and which he used for
his meditations was *The Imitation of Christ*, attributed today to Thomas à
Kempis, but in Ignatius' time to Jean Gerson, the one-time Chancellor of
the University of Paris, and which Ignatius affectionately called his "Little
Gerson." Later in life Ignatius stated: "It was at Manresa that I saw the
Gerçonzito for the first time, and since then there is no other book of devotion that I like more."[7] Though Ignatius was no longer plagued by scruples
he was not totally free of the devil's subtle activity, for when it was time
to sleep his mind filled with spiritual lights with the result that he was
losing the sleep he sorely needed. Knowing well that he had not disregarded
God during the day, but had given Him many hours in prayer and reflec-
tion, Ignatius concluded that these lights were but another manifestation
of the devil's wiles and thus cast them aside and slept the few hours he
had allotted himself.

as did wonderful consolations, so that they took up most of the time that he had set aside for sleep, which was not much. Now and then reflecting on this loss of sleep, he considered how he had allotted a fixed amount of time each day to converse with God, and then the remainder of the day as well, and thus he came to doubt whether those lights came from the good spirit. He concluded that it was better to set them aside and sleep the allotted time. This he did.

27. He continued in his resolve to abstain from eating meat, and was so firm in that decision that for nothing would he think of changing it. Then one morning, after he got out of bed, some meat appeared before him just as if he saw it with his body's eyes, though he had no prior craving for it. At the same time a powerful inclination of will came over him henceforth to eat meat. Though he remembered his earlier resolve, still he did not hesitate to decide that he ought to eat meat. Later on, when he related this to his confessor, the confessor told him to study the matter to see if, by chance, it was a temptation. After putting it through a thorough examination he was sure that it was not.

During this period God was dealing with him in the same

27. During his months in Manresa Ignatius sought spiritual guidance from many individuals but found none able to give him what he needed, and having gone through months of darkness of soul, he finally learned that his teacher in all this was our Lord Himself. Ignatius was but a child in the school of the spiritual life and it was our Lord who taught him how to discern the spirits that were moving him and enabled him to see that both the abstaining from meat and the eating of the same may be equally praiseworthy. In Christian tradition Ignatius is famous for his development of the art of the discernment of spirits. As a result of the diversity of spirits that he experienced at Loyola and at Manresa, he came to learn how to distinguish them, and thus came to know what was God's will for him. The knowledge that Ignatius gained from these experiences may be found in the Rules for the Discernment of Spirits in his Spiritual Exercises.

Of the many things that Ignatius learned under our Lord's guidance, he calls attention to five special graces granted him to indicate that it was time for his soul to pass from darkness into the light of mystical graces.

way a schoolteacher deals with a child while instructing him. This was because either he was thick and dull of brain, or because of the firm will that God Himself had implanted in him to serve Him — but he clearly recognized and has always recognized that it was in this way that God dealt with him. Furthermore, if he were to doubt this, he would think he was offending the Divine Majesty. One can see how God dealt with him in the following five examples.

28. First. He was greatly devoted to the Most Holy Trinity, and every day he prayed to each of the three Persons. But while doing the same to the Most Holy Trinity the thought came to him, why four prayers to the Trinity? But this thought caused him little or no trouble since it was of so little importance. One day, as he was saying the Hours of Our Lady on the monastery's steps, his understanding was raised on high, so as to see the Most Holy Trinity under the aspect of three keys on a musical instrument, and as a result he shed many tears and sobbed so strongly that he could not control himself. Joining in a procession that came out of the monastery, that morning he could not hold back his tears until dinnertime, and after he

28. The prayer books of the sixteenth century usually contained prayers directed to each of the three Persons of the Trinity, and then there was a fourth prayer directed not to any one of the Persons but to the Triune God. Ignatius wondered about the need for this fourth prayer but he also recognized that his question was of little importance. His reflections on the Trinity were soon to be resolved by an extraordinary grace. One morning, as he was about to enter the Dominican church and as his thoughts were focused on the Trinity, Ignatius was given to understand how the three distinct Persons in the Godhead could form a single unity. He saw the three divine Persons as three keys on an instrument. Each key has its own individual sound, but when the three keys are played together, each key, without losing any of its own distinctiveness, contributes itself and together the three form a unified harmonic chord. What Ignatius had learned that morning stayed with him that day so that he could do nothing else but think of the Trinity and talk about It. This experience indeed remained with him for the rest of his life as his *Spiritual Journal*[8] amply attests.

had eaten he could not refrain from talking, with much joy and consolation, about the Most Holy Trinity, making use of different comparisons. This experience remained with him for the rest of his life so that whenever he prayed to the Most Holy Trinity he felt great devotion.

29. Second. One day it was granted him to understand, with great spiritual joy, the way in which God had created the world. He seemed to see a white object with rays stemming from it, from which God made light. He neither knew how to explain these things nor did he fully remember the spiritual lights that God had then imprinted on his soul.

Third. It was likewise in Manresa—where he stayed for almost a year, and after experiencing divine consolations and seeing the fruit that he was bringing forth in the souls he was helping—that he abandoned those extremes he had previously practiced and began to cut his nails and hair. One day, while in town and attending Mass in the church attached to the above-mentioned monastery, he saw with inward eyes, at the time of the elevation of the body of the Lord, some white rays coming from above. But after so long a time he is now unable to adequately explain this; nevertheless, he clearly saw with his

29. Other exceptional mystical graces granted him were to behold how everything in creation proceeded from the Triune God and how Christ's body became present in the Eucharist at the words of consecration in the Mass. Ignatius was likewise granted interiorly to see Christ's humanity and that of our Lady, and he notes that this vision of Christ was of rather frequent occurrence, and not only in Manresa but also when he was traveling to Padua (see #41) and while in the Holy Land (see #48). So vivid and so powerful were these interior illuminations that Ignatius said he could not doubt their truthfulness and that he was even willing to give his life for them. All these graces came to him at the time that he was being sought after as a spiritual guide. Seeing that his contacts with other spiritual-minded persons were bearing fruit, and fearing that his appearance might be keeping some from visiting him and thus depriving them of the help he could offer them, Ignatius abandoned the extreme measures he adopted from Saint Onuphrius and once again cut his hair and nails.

understanding how our Lord Jesus Christ was present in that
most holy Sacrament.

Fourth. During prayer he often, and for an extended period
of time, saw with inward eyes the humanity of Christ, whose
form appeared to him as a white body, neither very large nor
very small; nor did he see any differentiation of members. He
often saw this in Manresa; and if he were to say twenty times
or forty times, he would not presume to say that he was lying.
He saw it again when he was in Jerusalem, and once more when
he was on his way to Padua. He has also seen our Lady in similar
form, without differentiation of members. These things that
he saw at that time fortified him and gave such great support
to his faith that many times he thought to himself: if there
were no Scriptures to teach us these matters of faith, he would
still resolve to die for them on the basis of what he had seen.

30. Fifth. He was once on his way, out of devotion, to a
church a little more than a mile from Manresa, which I think
was called Saint Paul. The road followed the path of the river
and he was taken up with his devotions; he sat down for a
while facing the river flowing far below him. As he sat there
the eyes of his understanding were opened and though he saw
no vision he understood and perceived many things, numerous

30-31. The fifth grace, and the most important, was the decisive moment in Ignatius' spiritual development. One day,[9] as he was walking toward
the church of Saint Paul the Hermit, a church attached to the Cistercian
monastery nearby,[10] Ignatius was caught up in his thoughts and sat down
on the shores of the Cardoner and continued his reflections. God flooded
his soul with extraordinary light, giving him a profound insight into and
feeling for the mysteries of the faith. Ignatius now understood these truths
with such a clarity that even though he had reflected on them in the past
they were as totally new to him. Furthermore, they were so encompassing
that what he had learned on that one occasion was more than he had learned since that event. Together with the broader understanding of the faith
Ignatius received a fuller realization of his vocation and possessed a clearer
determination to follow Christ. At the illumination's end, Ignatius went
a bit farther to the Cross of Tort, and there he spilled out his gratitude

spiritual things as well as matters touching on faith and learn-ing, and this was with an elucidation so bright that all these things seemed new to him. He cannot expound in detail what he then understood, for they were many things, but he can state that he received such a lucidity in understanding that during the course of his entire life — now having passed his sixty-second year — if he were to gather all the helps he received from God and everything he knew, and add them together, he does not think they would add up to all that he received on that one occasion.

31. And after this lasted for some time, he went to kneel before a cross, which was near that place, to give thanks to God, and there that vision appeared to him — the one that had appeared many times before and which he had never under-stood — that is, the object described earlier which seemed most beautiful to him, with its many eyes. Kneeling before the cross he noticed that the object was without the beautiful color it usually had, and he distinctly understood, and felt the firm agree-ment of his will, that that was the evil spirit. Many times later it continued to appear to him, but as a mark of his disdain for it he drove it away with the pilgrim's staff he always had in his hand.

32. On one occasion, while in Manresa, having fallen ill with a high fever and being on the point of death, he was quite cer-

to God for the graces granted him. It was while kneeling before that cross that the vision of the serpentine form (see #19) appeared, but in the light of his most recent enlightenment he quickly detected that that shiny form was the evil spirit, and whenever it again appeared Ignatius brandished his staff and the form disappeared.

Ignatius narrated this portion of his life's story to Father Gonçalves da Câmara sometime in March 1555, and since Ignatius gives his age as 62, it appears that he had been under the impression that he had been born in 1493.

32. Because of the severe penances that Ignatius was in the habit of prac-ticing, it is no wonder that he several times fell ill in Manresa. The incident

tain that his soul was about to depart his body. At that instant the thought came into his mind that he was numbered among the righteous, but this brought him so much distress that he tried everything to dismiss it and to dwell on his sins. He had more difficulty with that thought than with the fever, but no matter how he toiled to overcome it, he was unable to do so. When the fever lessened and he was no longer in danger of death, he loudly cried out to certain ladies who had come to visit him that the next time they saw him at death's door they were, for the love of God, to shout aloud that he was a sinner and that he should be ever mindful of the sins he had committed against God.

33. On another occasion, when he was traveling from Valencia to Italy by sea, the ship's rudder became smashed in a violent storm, and being in a crisis, he and many other passengers aboard concluded that, as things then stood, they would not be able to escape death. Thus, making use of his time, he made a careful

here recorded may have taken place during the summer of 1522. Ignatius had been praying at the shrine of Our Lady of Villadordis and was found unconscious by a passerby. He was taken to the hospital and from there the Amigrant family took him into its home and cared for him.[11] With his body burning with fever Ignatius was certain that death was soon to take him. The thought of death, however, did not cause him fear; in fact, the thought passed through his mind that he had nothing to fear since he was numbered among the just. This so disturbed him, probably fearing that this was yielding to vanity, that he tried to dismiss the thought by thinking of his sins, but he was unable to dispel it. When the fever had passed and after he had recognized those caring for him, he asked that if he ever again became ill they were to remind him that he was a sinner.

33. The remembrance of his nearness to death in Manresa led Ignatius to think of two other incidents in his life, and in both there was no fear but joy. The first took place in 1535 when he boarded a vessel in Valencia to go to Genoa—he was on his way to meet his companions in Venice, intending to go with them on pilgrimage to the Holy Land. The second was when Ignatius was in Rome and had been sick from the end of 1550 to the beginning of 1551.[12]

examination of conscience and prepared himself for death, but he felt no fear because of his sins nor was he afraid of being condemned, but he was especially disturbed and sorry, knowing that he had not put to good use all the gifts and graces that God our Lord had granted him.

In the year 1550, he was once more gravely ill, due to a serious sickness which, in his own judgment and that of others, was to be his last. Thinking of death at the time, he experienced such joy and so much spiritual consolation in the thought of having to die that he burst into tears. This came to be of such frequent occurrence that many times he stopped thinking of death just so as not to have so much consolation.

34. When winter came, he became sick with a severe illness and in order that he could recover the city placed him in the house of the father of a certain Ferrera, who later entered the service of Baltasar de Faria. There he was assiduously cared for and many important ladies, who were devoted to him, came to watch through the night. He recovered from his illness but he nevertheless remained weak and frequently suffered stomach pains. Because of his condition and because the winter was most severe, the ladies made him dress properly, wear shoes, and cover his head. Thus they made him accept two brown-colored jackets, made of very coarse cloth, and a beret of the same material as

---

34. Ignatius' final illness in Manresa was during the winter of 1522, and because he was so greatly esteemed the city saw that he had proper care and placed him in the house of Antonio Benito Ferrer.[13] Ignatius well remembered that family because Antonio's son later entered the service of Baltasar da Faria, who had been the King of Portugal's agent in Rome during the years 1543-1551.[14] The ladies[15] who cared for Ignatius decided that the simple rough tunic he had been wearing was less than sufficient to keep him warm during the wintry months and thus they imposed upon him to accept heavier clothes and suggested that if he dressed properly and covered his head he would reduce the chances of again becoming ill. Once Ignatius was able to get about and noted that spring was coming, his thoughts focused on Jerusalem.

a cap. During this time there were many days when he was most desirous to talk of spiritual matters and to find some individuals able to do so. But the time that he set for his departure for Jerusalem was fast approaching.

35. At the beginning of the year 1523, he departed for Barcelona in order to set sail, and though some individuals offered to accompany him, he wanted to go by himself for his desire was to have only God as his refuge. One day, as his friends were pressing him to take a companion, telling him how helpful a companion would be, since he knew neither Italian nor Latin, and commending one, he answered that even if it were the son or brother of the Duke of Cardona he would not travel with him because he wanted to exercise the virtues of charity, of faith, and of hope. By taking a companion he would expect help from him when he was hungry, and if he should fall, he would expect him to help him get up; consequently he would put his trust in the companion and have affection for him, but he wanted to place his trust, love, and hope in God alone. What he thus said came right from his heart. It was with such a disposition that he wanted to set sail, not only by himself but also without provisions. In arranging for his passage he convinced the ship's captain to give him free passage, since he had no money, but on condition that he bring with him enough biscuit to last him through the journey. In no other way in the world would they take him on board.

35. After having spent ten months in Manresa, Ignatius left the city in mid-February 1523.[16] Once arrived in Barcelona he went to the residence of Inés Pascual,[17] whom he had known in Manresa and whose house was near the harbor. Ignatius' friends knew that he was seeking passage to Italy but they interpreted this to mean that he was merely going to Rome. They tried to persuade him to take a companion since he knew neither Latin nor Italian, but he wanted his pilgrimage to be an expression of complete trust in God. In mentioning the Duke of Cardona, Ignatius does so not only because the duke belonged to one of the noblest families in Catalonia, but also because he knew the duke's sister, Juana, for she was the wife of his former master, the Duke of Nájera.

36. When he was arranging for the biscuit, he began to have great scruples. "Is this the hope and faith you have in the God who would not fail you?" And so on. These thoughts were so persistent that they caused him great distress. Finally, not knowing what he should do because he saw good reasons on both sides, he decided to place himself in the hands of his confessor. He thus told him how greatly he desired to seek perfection and what was for the greater glory of God, as well as the reasons that made him hesitate about taking provisions with him. The confessor decided that he should beg for whatever he needed and to take it with him. As he was begging from a lady, she asked him where he intended to go. At first he hesitated to tell her, but finally said that he was going to Italy and Rome, not daring to say any more. Somewhat astonished, she said: "You want to go to Rome? As for those who go there, no one knows how they will return?" By this she meant that those who go to Rome return with little spiritual profit. The reason why he did not dare to say that he was going to Jerusalem was his fear of vainglory; this fear so plagued him

36-37. The ship's captain was willing to give Ignatius free passage, but he insisted that Ignatius had to bring his own provisions. Ignatius saw this as being in conflict with his desire to have full dependence upon God, but his confessor convinced him that by begging the money for his provisions he would still be trusting in God. Ignatius approached a certain lady for alms, and when she asked where he was heading, she was somewhat startled that it should be Rome for she was convinced that all who visited Rome returned in a worse moral condition than when they departed. This lady is sometimes identified as Isabel Roser,[18] who later became one of Ignatius' closest friends and greatest benefactors. With the money he collected he bought his supply of biscuit and the few *blancas* he had in his pocket — they were coins of the lowest denomination then in use — he left on a bench for any passerby to pick up.

In Barcelona, as in Manresa, Ignatius attempted to single out spiritual individuals, but over the past months the only one whom he considered to have made progress in the spiritual life was the elderly woman mentioned in #21. After three weeks in Barcelona Ignatius was ready to sail for Italy.

that he never dared to say from what country he came, nor
who his family was. Finally, having obtained the biscuit, he
got ready to go aboard. Arriving at the ship, he found that
he still had five or six *blancas* left of what he had received begging from door to door—for this was his usual way of support-
ing himself—and he left the coins on a bench that he found
near the shore.

37. After having been in Barcelona a little more than twenty
days, he went aboard ship. But while still in Barcelona and before
boarding ship, he followed his usual custom of searching out
spiritual persons in order to talk to them, and even visited those
living in hermitages far from the city. But neither in Barcelona
nor in Manresa—for the entire time that he was there—was
he able to find individuals who were able to help him as much
as he desired. Only in Manresa, that woman we have already
mentioned, who told him that she had prayed to God that Jesus
Christ appear to him, she alone seemed to him to have made
progress in the spiritual life. Thus, after he left Barcelona, he
completely lost eagerness to search out spiritual persons.

Chapter 4

Jerusalem: Pilgrim in the Holy Land
(Mid-March–September 22, 1523)

38. With a strong wind behind them, they made the trip from Barcelona to Gaeta in five days and five nights, with everyone still fearful because of the severe storm. Everywhere in that region there was fear of the plague, but as soon as he disembarked he started walking toward Rome. From among those who were aboard ship, a mother and her daughter, who was dressed in boy's clothing, joined him, as did another young man. They accompanied him because they too were begging their way. When they arrived at a large farmhouse they found a big fire and around it many soldiers who offered them something to eat and gave them much wine, persuading them to drink on, as if, it seemed, they wanted to get them drunk. Then they separated; the mother and daughter went to an upstairs room, while the pilgrim and the young man went to a stable. In the middle of the night he heard loud shouts coming from upstairs and rising to see what the noise was, he found the mother and daughter in tears in the courtyard below, weeping and lamenting because the soldiers had tried to violate them.

38. The vessel carrying Ignatius left Barcelona in mid-March 1523, and since Gaeta, Italy, is almost due east of Barcelona, the vessel traveled something of a straight line, passing through the Strait of Bonifacio which separates Corsica from Sardinia. Because of favorable winds the crossing took only five days and nights, and Ignatius arrived in Italy about March 20-22. Gaeta is situated approximately seventy-five miles south of Rome and fifty miles north of Naples.

So strong an emotion took hold of him that he began to shout out: "Do we have to put up with this?" and similar complaints which he uttered with such effectiveness that everyone was so dumbfounded that no one laid a hand on him. The young man had already fled, so the three of them continued their journey, though it was still night.

39. When they arrived at a nearby city, they found the gates closed, and being unable to enter, all three of them spent that night in a church dank from the rain and located outside the city. When morning came the city was closed to them, and because they found no alms outside they went to a castle which was not far away. There the pilgrim became weak — as much from the trials at sea as from others — and not being able to continue his way he remained there while the mother and daughter made for Rome. That day many people came out of the city and learning that the first lady of that region had also come out, he presented himself before her to tell her that his

39. Since the plague was of somewhat frequent occurrence in the sixteenth century, and because it brought many deaths with it, Italian cities were especially careful about admitting strangers within their walls without certificates attesting to their good health. Thus, when Ignatius arrived at this city north of Gaeta he found the city gates closed and was not permitted to enter. The name of that city has not come down to us, but since it was near Gaeta, two cities have been suggested. Some authors think that because the lady in question understood Ignatius she herself must have been Spanish, and thus they suggest that the lady was Juana of Aragón, the wife of Ascanio Colonna, whose seat was in Paliano. On the other hand, it would not be altogether impossible for an educated Italian lady to understand the simple question that Ignatius had proposed to her, and hence other authors suggest that the lady was Beatrice Appiani, wife of Vespasiano Colonna, whose seat was at Fondi.[1]

The *quattrini* that Ignatius collected were coins of the smallest denomination then in use in Italy; they would be like our pennies today. The usual route from Gaeta to Rome went through Velletri, and the distance was about seventy-five miles. Since Ignatius arrived in Rome on Palm Sunday, we have a definite date for his entrance into the Eternal City. In 1523, Palm Sunday was celebrated on March 29.

only infirmity was weakness and asked her permission to enter the city to seek some medicine. She promptly granted his request. He started begging in the city and collected a good supply of *quattrini*. Feeling his health return after two days, he continued his journey and arrived in Rome on Palm Sunday.

40. Everyone who spoke to him in Rome, knowing that he had no money to go to Jerusalem, tried to talk him out of his trip, offering him all kinds of reasons why it would be impossible for him to find a free passage. But he felt a firm certainty within his soul that he would find a way of going to Jerusalem, and of this he had no doubt. After he had received the blessing of Pope Hadrian VI, he then set out for Venice, some eight or nine days after the feast of the Resurrection. He also took with him six or seven ducats which he had received for his passage from Venice to Jerusalem, and these he had ac-

---

40. It was customary for pilgrims to the Holy Land to first receive the pope's permission and benediction before starting out. Ignatius received his permission on March 31, two days after his arrival in Rome. A record of this permission is still preserved in the Vatican Archives, and Ignatius is there referred to as "Iñigo of Loyola, cleric of the Diocese of Pamplona."[2] When Pope Hadrian VI, a Dutchman and former tutor of Charles V, was elected to the Chair of Saint Peter on January 9, 1522, he had been residing in Spain and had been the country's Prime Minister. He came to Rome in August of that year, several months before Ignatius visited the city, and was to die on September 14, 1523, five months after Ignatius departed Rome.

The friends with whom Ignatius talked in Rome were most probably Spaniards whom he met in the Spanish district of Rome near the Piazza Navona, and it was probably these friends who had taken up a collection among themselves and had given him a gift of six or seven ducats to help defray the expenses of his passage to Jerusalem. Several ducats were but a beginning toward the amount he needed for his passage; nevertheless, he felt that having these ducats in his pocket was a denial of his former hope that God would get him there. Ignatius spent Holy Week in Rome and sometime during his two-week stay he visited the city's major basilicas. Since Easter that year was on April 5, and since Ignatius informs us that he left Rome eight or nine days later, it would then seem that he began his journey to Venice about April 13 or 14.

cepted only because he was overcome by the fear they had implanted in him by saying that there was absolutely no other
way of getting there. Two days after leaving Rome he began
thinking that this showed a lack of confidence in God, and the
taking of those ducats so disturbed him that he thought it would
be good to be finished with them. He decided, in the end, to
give them with open hands to those he might meet on the way,
who were usually the poor. This he did in such a way that
when he arrived in Venice he had only a few *quattrini* with him,
and he needed those for that night.

41. On his way to Venice, he slept outside under arches
because of the restrictions then in force due to the plague. Once
it happened that one morning as he was getting up he bumped
into a man who, as soon as he saw him, fled in great fright
because he must have had a very pale look about him.

Walking, he reached Chioggia, and from some of the companions who had joined him he learned that they would not
be allowed to enter Venice. The companions decided to go to
Padua and there get health certificates, and so he went along
with them. Since he could not walk as they did—they were
walking at a quick pace—they left him in a large field as night
was coming on. While in the field Christ appeared to him in
the way that He usually appeared to him, as we have already
stated, and this brought him great comfort. The next morning, still experiencing this consolation, he arrived at Padua's

41. The route that Ignatius followed from Rome to Venice is not
known, but the more likely route was to pass through the cities of Narni,
Terni, and Spoleto, then head for Ancona on the coast, and then turn north-
ward, passing through Rimini, Ravenna, Ferrara, and finally Chioggia,
which is located at the entrance of the lagoon and only some fifteen miles
from Venice.[3] Ignatius' vision of Christ in the field near Padua was similar
to the visions he had in Manresa (see #29), and was granted him to indicate
that his pilgrimage was under our Lord's protection and that he need not
worry about minor details such as health certificates and money for his
passage.

gates and without forging any certificate, as I believe his companions had done, he entered the city without the guards asking anything of him. The same thing happened as he left the city, and this especially surprised his companions since they had come to procure these certificates in order to go to Venice, while he showed no interest in getting one for himself.

42. When they arrived in Venice, inspectors came to the boat to check everyone, one by one, as many as were on board. But they left him alone. In Venice he supported himself by begging and he slept in Saint Mark's Square. He did not want to go to the residence of the emperor's ambassador, nor did he make any special effort to find the means to pay for his passage. He enjoyed a great certainty of soul that God would provide the means for getting to Jerusalem and this feeling so strengthened his resolve that no reason or fear suggested to him could make him waver.

One day, he came across a rich Spaniard who asked him what he was doing there and where he wanted to go. Learning of his plans, the Spaniard took him home for a meal and then kept him there for some days until his departure was arranged. Ever since his days in Manresa the pilgrim had the custom that when he was eating with others he never talked at table, except to give brief answers. But he listened to all that was said and mentally noted certain items which he would later use in speaking about God. When the meal was over, he then joined in the conversation.

42. After a four-week walk and a short boat trip, Ignatius arrived in Venice about mid-May 1523. Because Venice, the capital of The Most Serene Republic, was an important seaport and controlled the Adriatic and a good portion of the Mediterranean Sea, it was she that handled the pilgrim trade to the Holy Land. Upon Ignatius' arrival in Venice, he spent his first night in a hospice, but the following nights he slept under the pillared collonades of Saint Mark's Square. Since his trust was entirely in God, he saw no need to seek help from the Spanish ambassador, who at that time was Alonso Sánchez. The kind Spaniard who had taken Ignatius into his home until his departure for Jerusalem remains unknown.[4]

43. For this reason the good man and his entire household grew so fond of him, that they desired him to stay with them and tried to keep him there. His host took him to the Doge of Venice so that he could speak with him, that is, he arranged an entry and an audience with him. The doge listened to the pilgrim and gave instructions that he be given passage on the ship taking the governors to Cyprus.

Though many pilgrims had come that year on their way to Jerusalem, most of them had returned to their homeland because of the recent capture of Rhodes. Still, there were thirteen on the pilgrim ship, which was the first to depart, and eight or nine others waited for the governors' ship. While waiting to set sail, a very high fever struck our pilgrim and after it had made him quite ill for a few days it then left him. The ship set sail the very day that he had taken a purgative. Those of the household asked the physician if he would be able to embark for Jerusalem, and the physician answered that he certainly could leave for Jerusalem to be buried there. That day he boarded ship and set sail; he vomited a great deal but found himself relieved and soon he was on the road to recovery. On that ship some individuals engaged in openly lewd and obscene behavior, which he severely condemned.

43. The doge who gave Ignatius free passage to Cyprus was Andrea Gritti (1455-1538), who had been elected to that office on May 10, 1523,[5] just four days before Ignatius arrived in Venice. Because of the recent fall of Rhodes to the Turks in December 1522, there were only twenty-one pilgrims in the city, and since this number was much too small for the scheduled *Pilgrim Galley* to set sail, the pilgrims were placed on two merchant vessels. Thirteen were put aboard the smaller of the two, which Ignatius calls the "pilgrim ship," while the remaining eight, including our pilgrim, were on the *Negrona*. Since the island of Cyprus had but recently come under the control of Venice, new governors were being sent to the island and to its three ports, Limassol, Larnaca, and Famagusta. The pilgrim ship set sail on June 29, 1523,[6] and the *Negrona* left Venice on July 14.[7]

44. The Spaniards traveling with him advised him not to speak out, because the crew was considering depositing him

44. Though Ignatius never kept a diary of his pilgrimage to the Holy Land, nor did he describe any of its details, nevertheless two of the pilgrims on that 1523 journey did keep diaries and from them we can construct a chronology.[8] The diarists were Philip Hagen, a gentleman from Strasbourg, aboard the pilgrim ship, and Peter Füssli, a bell-founder from Zurich, aboard the *Negrona*. Besides Hagen, there was on the pilgrim ship, another German as well as eleven pilgrims from Brabant and Holland; on the *Negrona*, in addition to Ignatius and Füssli, there were two more Swiss, a Tyrolese, and three Spaniards. Among these Spaniards was an unidentified priest, and Diego Manes, Commander of the Order of Saint John, and his servant. For Ignatius to have remembered the commander's name after thirty years seems to indicate that he must have been sufficiently impressed by him. These were the Spaniards who kindly told Ignatius to close his eyes to the misbehavior taking place on the ship's deck. The *Negrona* carried a crew of thirty-two and many passengers—government officials with their families and servants, as well as traders and merchants.

After the *Negrona* had left Venice it followed the Dalmatian coast, stopping at Rovigno and then in a bay near Pola to weather a storm; on August 1, Albania was in sight and then there was a stop at Candia in Crete and finally on August 14, after a month at sea, the *Negrona* docked at Famagusta in Cyprus, where the governors disembarked. Benedetto Ragazzoni, the ship's captain, was scheduled to continue the voyage to Beirut, and the eight pilgrims were to disembark there and travel overland down to Galilee and then southward to Jerusalem. But because of the plague then afflicting Beirut, Ragazzoni discontinued his voyage. Consequently, the eight pilgrims had to leave the *Negrona* in Famagusta and walk the thirty miles to Las Salinas (modern Larnaca), where they met the pilgrim ship that had left Venice two weeks ahead of them. Captain Jacopo Alberto was of a mind to abandon his thirteen pilgrims in Cyprus but when the additional eight arrived from the *Negrona* and after they had agreed to pay twenty ducats each for passage to Jaffa with a return to Cyprus, Alberto agreed to take them aboard. Since the captain was making a profit on this deal he gave Ignatius free passage, and the pilgrim ship set sail on August 19.

According to the diarists, the vessel came into sight of Jaffa on August 22, but because of a pilot's error they went further southward and then, delayed by a storm, they did not arrive at Jaffa until August 25, a Tuesday.

on some island or other. But our Lord saw to it that they arrived speedily at Cyprus, where they left the ship and went overland to another port named Las Salinas, about ten leagues away. There they boarded the pilgrim ship and he took nothing with him as rations except his confidence in God, just as he had done on the other ship. During this period our Lord appeared to him on many occasions, giving him much strength and consolation. It seemed to him that he saw a large round object, as though it were of gold, and this frequently appeared to him from the time they left Cyprus to the time they arrived at Jaffa. Making their way to Jerusalem on small donkeys, as was the custom, a Spaniard, a nobleman by his appearance, named Diego Manes, about two miles outside Jerusalem devoutly suggested to the pilgrims that since they would shortly be arriving at the point where they would be able to see the Holy City, it would be good for all of them to prepare their consciences and proceed in silence.

45. Since this seemed agreeable to all, each one recollected himself, and a little before they arrived at the place whence they

Before the pilgrims were able to disembark, the captain had to go to Ramle to inform the Franciscan friars, who had charge of the Holy Places, that the pilgrims had arrived, and to Jerusalem to request safe conduct and a Turkish escort for them. The pilgrims first set foot in the Holy Land on August 31 and walked to the escort awaiting them. The distance from Jaffa to Jerusalem is only thirty-five miles, but because of Turkish rough handling and harassment it took the twenty-one pilgrims four days to cover that short distance.

45. The pilgrims had their first sight of Jerusalem on September 4, and entering the Holy City through the Jaffa Gate, they were housed in the Hospital of Saint John, near the church of the Holy Sepulcher, the usual residence for pilgrims. The following day, September 5, with their Franciscan guide, the pilgrims followed the traditional itinerary in visiting the Holy Places in Jerusalem, e.g., Mount Sion, the Upper Room where our Lord washed the feet of His disciples, the column of the flagellation, the convent of the Dormition of Our Lady, the residences of Annas, Caiaphas, and Pilate, now converted into chapels, as well as the church of the Holy

could get a glimpse of the city, they dismounted because they noticed friars waiting for them with a cross. When the pilgrim did see the city, he experienced great consolation, and all the others affirmed the same, saying that they all felt a joy that did not seem natural. He felt this same devotion on all his visits to the Holy Places.

He made a firm decision to remain in Jerusalem, constantly visiting the Holy Places. In addition to this devout desire of his, he was also intent on helping souls, and for this purpose he had with him letters of recommendation to the guardian. Handing them over to him, he informed the guardian of his intention to remain there because of his devotion, but said nothing of his other desire to help souls. He often and openly spoke to others about his wanting to remain, but to no one did he mention his second desire. The guardian replied that he did not see how he could possibly stay since the convent was in such dire need that it could not even support the friars living there, and that was why he had determined to send some of them back home together with the pilgrims. The pilgrim answered that he wanted nothing from the convent, but only

Sepulcher. On the 6th, a Sunday, everyone attended Mass in that same church and received Holy Communion, and that afternoon they participated in the Way of the Cross. On the 7th they visited Bethany and the Mount of Olives; on the 8th and 9th they were in Bethlehem. They spent the 10th visiting the valley of Jehosaphat and the brook Kedron, and the entire night of the 11th was spent within the church of the Holy Sepulcher. September 12-13 were days of rest and on the 14th they went to Jericho and to the Jordan, where some took baths and where everyone drank of its water. Because 500 Turkish cavalry arrived in Jerusalem from Damascus on September 16, the pilgrims were advised not to appear in the streets and thus they remained in relative seclusion until September 23.[9]

Sometime during his stay Ignatius visited the superior of the Franciscan monastery of Mount Sion in Jerusalem, and made known to him his desire to remain behind. The Father Guardian, however, felt that he himself could not grant the pilgrim that permission and said that it would have to wait until the provincial returned from Bethlehem.

that when he should come there for confession, they would hear him. This the guardian said he could do, but he would have to wait until the provincial (I think he was the head of the Order in that country) returned from visiting Bethlehem.

46. Finding assurance in this promise, the pilgrim began writing letters to spiritual persons back in Barcelona. After he had written one and was in the process of writing another — it was the eve of the pilgrims' departure — he was summoned by the guardian and the provincial, who had just returned. The provincial told him most kindly that he knew of his good intentions to remain in the Holy Places and that he had given much thought to this matter; nevertheless, because of his experience with others he judged that it was not a good idea. Many others had had the same desire, and some of them had been taken prisoner and some of them had been killed; his religious Order was later obliged to ransom those in captivity. Therefore, he should be ready to leave with the other pilgrims on the following day. He replied that his decision to remain was fixed and that nothing could prevent him from carrying it out. With great honesty he gave the provincial to understand that though the provincial did not agree with him, and since this was not a matter that obliged under sin, he would not renounce his plans out of fear. In answer to this the pro-

46-48. Ignatius had his visit with the Franciscan provincial on September 22, and having heard that the provincial possessed full authority, granted him by Rome, to decide who could remain in Jerusalem, our pilgrim immediately obeyed. But now that he would have to depart, he revisited the Mount of Olives. The stone from which our Lord ascended into heaven is still preserved there; the print of the left foot has been almost entirely erased by the devout kisses of pilgrims, but that of the right foot is still somewhat clear.[10] The servant whom the Franciscans sent looking for Ignatius presumably wore a special belt or carried some mark on his belt indicating that he was a Christian[11] or that he was associated with the custody of the Holy Places. Having returned to the hospice, Ignatius prepared to leave the Holy Land.

vincial said that they had authority from the Apostolic See to expel or to keep anyone they chose, and to excommunicate anyone who refused to obey, and in his case they were of the opinion that he should not remain, and so forth.

47. The provincial was willing to show him the bulls empowering them to excommunicate, but he said he had no need to see them since he believed their reverences, and since they arrived at their decision in accordance with the authority they possessed, he would obey them. When this was all over he returned to the place where he was staying. Since it was not our Lord's will for him to remain in the Holy Places, a burning desire took hold of him to make a return visit to the Mount of Olives before leaving. On the Mount of Olives there is a stone from which our Lord ascended into heaven, and his footprints are still visible there. This was what he again wanted to see. Thus, without saying anything, and without taking a guide (for those who go about without a Turk as guide run great risks), he slipped away from the others and went by himself to the Mount of Olives. The guards there did not want to let him enter but he gave them a penknife that he had with him. After he had said his prayers with heartfelt consolation he got the desire to go to Bethphage. While there he remembered that on the Mount of Olives he had not taken full notice of the direction in which the right foot was pointing and which way the left. On his return there he gave his scissors, I think, to the guards so that they would let him enter.

48. When the monastery learned that he had left without a guide, the friars made every effort to find him. As he was coming down from the Mount of Olives he met a Christian of the Girdle who worked at the monastery; the Christian was carrying a large staff and, showing his great annoyance, waved it as if he were about to beat him up. When he came up to him, the servant vigorously grabbed him by the arm and he easily let himself be led away. The good man never let him go. Going along the road, held tightly by the Christian, our

Lord granted him great consolation and it seemed to him that he saw Christ above him the whole way. This consolation remained with him in great measure until he arrived at the monastery.

Chapter 5

Cyprus–Genoa: The Pilgrim's Return
(September 23, 1523–February 1524)

49. They set out the next day and after arriving in Cyprus the pilgrims separated, boarding different ships. There were

49. The pilgrims left Jerusalem on the night of September 23, 1523. On their way to Jaffa they were attacked by bedouins who stole their food, and when they arrived at Ramle, Turks locked them up for three days without food and water. The group finally arrived in Jaffa on October 2, and on the following day was on its way to Cyprus, landing at Las Salinas on the 14th.[1]

Since the *Negrona*, the vessel that brought them to Cyprus, had already left, the pilgrims were forced to seek alternate means of returning to Venice. Ignatius' companions tried to get him passage on the large Venetian ship then in port, but its shipmaster refused to take the poor pilgrim aboard. Though they praised Ignatius and spoke of his holiness, this was insufficient for the shipmaster, who retorted that if he were that holy he should travel as Saint James had traveled. Legend has it that after the saint's death in Jerusalem his body was placed on a ship that miraculously spread its sails and took the body to northern Spain, thus explaining how the apostle's body got to Santiago de Compostela.

While Ignatius was given free passage on the small ship, whose name has not been preserved, the diarists Füssli and Hagen had passage on the large vessel, and since Ignatius was no longer in their company the diaries that both men kept of their homeward voyage are not helpful to us.[2] Of the three ships that set sail for Venice in early November only the small one arrived. The unusually long voyage of two-and-a-half months would indicate that the vessel must have met several storms and squalls in its journey. Ignatius merely says that the vessel had met with difficulty, and the stopover on Italy's eastern shore was due to the bad weather.

three or four ships in port going to Venice: one was Turkish, another was a very small vessel, and the third was splendid and sturdy and was owned by a wealthy Venetian. Some pilgrims asked the shipmaster of this last ship if he would be willing to take the pilgrim on board, but learning that he had no money he would not, though many begged him to do so and spoke highly of the pilgrim. The shipmaster answered that if he were a saint he could travel as Saint James traveled, or something similar. These same petitioners easily received a favorable response from the master of the small ship. They set sail one day, in the morning, with a good wind, but by afternoon a storm rose and the ships were scattered. The large vessel was lost off the island of Cyprus and only its passengers were saved, while the Turkish ship and all passengers went down in the same storm. The small ship underwent much difficulty but, finally, it touched land in Apulia. It was when winter was at its worst, with snow and freezing temperatures. The pilgrim had no clothes other than a pair of breeches of rough cloth reaching his knees, with his legs left bare. He had shoes and a doublet of black material, torn at the shoulders, and a short loose coat that was threadbare.

50. He arrived in Venice in mid-January 1524, having been at sea, since leaving Cyprus, the entire months of November

50. Upon Ignatius' return to Venice, he met one of the two gentlemen who had befriended him prior to his trip to the Holy Land. This gentleman is usually identified as Marcantonio Trevisano, a Venetian senator, whose palace was located behind Saint Mark's Basilica.[3] The *giulii* that he gave Ignatius were silver coins minted during the pontificate of Pope Julius II (1503-1513), and were still in circulation, each worth about 1/10 of a ducat. Ignatius spent two weeks in Venice considering what he ought to do with his life now that he had to return from Jerusalem. He could still help others, but to be of greater assistance he determined that he should do some studying and thus he decided to go to Barcelona. He left Venice in early February and was soon in Ferrara where, while praying in the Cathedral of Saint George, beggars approached him for alms and with his usual generosity he gave away all that he had, leaving himself as poor as those who had come to him.

and December and half of January. In Venice he met one of the two gentlemen who had taken him into their homes before he departed for Jerusalem; the gentleman gave him an alms of fifteen or sixteen *giulii* and a piece of cloth that he folded several times over and placed over his abdomen because of the severe cold.

After the said pilgrim came to realize that it was God's will that he was not to remain in Jerusalem, he kept wondering what he ought to do and finally he was inclined toward spending some time in studies in order to help souls; and so he decided to go to Barcelona. Thus he left Venice for Genoa. One day, while in Ferrara's main church, finishing his devotions, a poor man asked him for an alms and he gave him a *marchetto*, that is, a coin worth five or six *quattrini*. After him another poor man came and he also gave him a small coin but of greater value. Then to a third, having only *giulii* left, he gave a *giulio*. Since the poor people saw him dispensing alms, they kept on coming until he gave away all that he had. Finally, many poor people came in a group requesting alms, but he asked their pardon, saying he had nothing left.

51. Then he left Ferrara for Genoa. On the way he met some Spanish soldiers who treated him well that night. They were quite surprised that he was traveling that road because it passed almost in the exact middle between the French and imperial armies. The soldiers suggested that he leave the highway and take another and safer road which they pointed out to him,

51-53. Among the various incidents that happened during Ignatius' journey from Ferrara to Genoa, three remained in his memory. France and Spain were at war in a dispute over Milan, but in early 1524, when Ignatius was crossing northern Italy, hostilities were fortunately at a standstill. At some unknown location Ignatius encountered Spanish soldiers; recognizing the traveler as a fellow countryman, the soldiers helped him in every way they could and even showed him what road to follow to avoid the French. But Ignatius, preferring to place his confidence in God, purposely continued on the highway. He walked all day and that evening he was seized as a spy, searched, and interrogated. Ignatius found spiritual

but he did not follow their advice. Walking straight ahead on the same road he came upon a town that had been burned and destroyed, and until that night he found no one to give him anything to eat. At sunset he came to a walled town where the guards immediately seized him, thinking he was a spy. They put him in a small hut next to the town's gate and questioned him, as they usually did those whom they suspected. He answered all their questions, saying that he knew nothing. They stripped him and searched his entire body down to his shoes, to see if he were carrying any letters. Unable to learn anything by these means, they bound him in order to take him to their captain, who would make him talk. He asked that they take him wearing his coat, but they refused to give it to him, and took him only in his breeches and doublet, which were mentioned earlier.

52. While on his way, the pilgrim had a representation of how Christ was led away, but this was not a vision as the others were. He was led down three main streets, and went without sadness but with joy and satisfaction. He was in the habit of addressing all whom he met in the familiar "you" form, and kept to this practice because it was in this way that Christ and the apostles spoke, and so forth. Passing through these streets, the thought came to him, together with thoughts of torture that they could inflict on him, that it would be good for him

consolation in this incident for now he had the chance to imitate his Master, who also had been arrested. Having been set free, Ignatius was soon again apprehended, but because the French captain was also a Basque, he permitted Ignatius to continue on his way.

When Ignatius arrived in Genoa, God's providence in his behalf was again made manifest. He unexpectedly came upon Rodrigo Portuondo, general in charge of the Spanish galleys.[4] Ignatius had known him since his days in the service of the Duke of Nájera, and had met him when the duke and his retinue visited the royal court. Portuondo easily arranged for Ignatius to board one of the ships going to Barcelona and though Andrea Doria, the famous Genoese admiral — now serving the French king — had pursued the Spanish vessel, he failed to capture it.

to drop that custom on this occasion and speak to the captain in the more formal and polite manner. But he immediately perceived that this was a temptation and said: "Since it is, I will not speak to him in the formal and dignified manner, nor will I show him any mark of respect, nor will I take my cap off to him."

53. When they came to the captain's quarters they left him in a lower room and in a little while the captain came and spoke with him. Without showing any mark of courtesy, he answered in few words with long pauses between them. The captain took him for a madman and instructed those who had brought him in: "This man has no brains; give him his belongings and throw him out." Leaving the residence, he soon met a Spaniard who lived in that city and who took him to his home and gave him something to eat after many hours of not eating, and all that he needed for the night. When morning came he set out and walked until late afternoon, when two soldiers in a tower noticed him and came down to apprehend him. They led him to their captain, who was a Frenchman. The captain asked him, among other things, from what country he came, and learning that he came from Guipúzcoa, he said: "I come from near there," seemingly from the neighborhood of Bayonne, and he continued: "Take him, give him something to eat, and treat him kindly."

On this journey from Ferrara to Genoa, many other less interesting things happened, and finally he arrived in Genoa, where a Basque named Portundo recognized him. On many occasions he had spoken to him when the pilgrim served at the court of the Catholic King. This man secured passage for him on a ship going to Barcelona and which ran great danger of being captured by Andrea Doria, who was then in the service of the French, and who had given them chase.

Chapter 6

Barcelona and Alcalá: Student Days
(February/March 1524–June 21, 1527)

54. After he had arrived in Barcelona, he informed Isabel Roser and Master Ardévol, who was then teaching grammar, of his desire to study. The idea seemed good to both of them; he offered to teach him without charge and she offered to supply him with whatever he needed to support himself. The pilgrim

54-55. Ignatius asserts (see #57) that he arrived in Barcelona during Lent 1524. That year Ash Wednesday was on February 9,[1] and since he had departed Venice sometime at the beginning of February and had walked across northern Italy and had taken a ship to Barcelona, he probably arrived in that city in the latter part of February or early March. He renewed his acquaintance with Isabel Roser[2] and it was she who introduced him to Master Jerónimo Ardévol. The studies that Ignatius especially wanted to pursue were in Christian perfection, and with this in mind he went to Manresa to put himself under the tutelage of a monk whom he had previously known at the Cistercian monastery of Saint Paul the Hermit.[3] Having learned that the monk had died, Ignatius returned to Barcelona and accepted the assistance that Roser and Ardévol had offered him. In the beginning Ardévol gave Ignatius private instruction, but when the former accepted a position at the University of Barcelona he invited Ignatius to sit in his classes — a thirty-four-year-old sitting among teenage boys.[4] The rudiments of Latin did not come easily to Ignatius. When he tried to memorize its various declensions and conjugations spiritual lights filled his mind pulling him away from his studies, but once he acknowledged that these thoughts came from the evil spirit, he was no longer troubled by them. With his usual openness Ignatius spoke to his teacher about his lack of progress, but now that he had discovered the cause of his problem he promised to put forth his best efforts. The church of Our Lady of the Sea was located near the port and was near Ardévol's residence.

knew a friar in Manresa, I think of the Order of Saint Bernard, a very spiritual man, and he wished to stay with him in order to learn how he could more easily give himself to the spirit, and how to be of help to souls. So he answered that he would accept their offer if in Manresa he did not find the spiritual profit he hoped to find. When he went there he found that the friar had died, and returning to Barcelona, he began his studies with great diligence. But one thing was proving a great hindrance to him and that was that whenever he tried to memorize anything, as is necessary in the early stages of grammar study, new understandings of spiritual things and new delights came to him, and in such a way that he could neither memorize anything nor could he rid himself of them, no matter how much he tried.

55. Giving much thought to this matter, he said to himself: "Even when I am at prayer or at Mass, such clear understandings do not come to me!" Then, little by little, he came to recognize that these were temptations. After saying a prayer, he went to Our Lady of the Sea, near his teacher's house, having asked him to meet him in the church and hear him out. While they were seated together, he faithfully described to his teacher all that was going on in his soul, how little progress he had made until then, and for what reason. But he made a promise to his teacher, saying: "I promise you, that as long as I can find bread and water in Barcelona to support myself, I will never miss any of your classes during these two years." Since he made this promise with great earnestness, he never

During Ignatius' two years in Barcelona he lodged with the widow Inés Pascual,[5] whom he had met in Manresa, and who had a little shop in Barcelona, near the church of Our Lady of the Sea, and had her living quarters above the shop. Ignatius' room was there, but for his daily bread he went begging in the streets of Barcelona. He continued to devote a specified amount of time to prayer and he likewise continued his practice of penance. But to disguise this fact he made holes in his shoes so that he could feel the rough cobblestones as he made his way through the city.

again had those temptations. The stomach pain, which he first had in Manresa and which was the reason why he wore shoes, now left him, and he found his stomach feeling as well as when he left for Jerusalem. This was the reason why, during his studies in Barcelona, the desire to resume his former penances returned to him. He made holes in the soles of his shoes and kept enlarging them little by little, so that when winter's cold came there was nothing there but the upper part of the shoes.

56. After he completed two years of study and after having been told that he had made great progress in them, his teacher told him that he was now ready to pursue the liberal arts and that he should go to Alcalá. Notwithstanding, he had a doctor in theology examine him and he gave him the same advice. He set out alone for Alcalá, though I believe he already had some followers. Upon his arrival in Alcalá, he began begging and living on alms. One day, after living in this manner for some ten or twelve days, a cleric and others with him, seeing him begging, began to make fun of him and uttered some insulting remarks, as it frequently happens when someone healthy is seen begging. At that moment the gentleman in charge of

56. After two years of basic Latin Ignatius was prepared for advanced work and so Master Ardévol suggested that he go to the University of Alcalá. During his stay in Barcelona he found three individuals who, like him, were interested in helping souls and these three, Calixto de Sa,[6] Lope de Cáceres,[7] and Juan de Arteaga,[8] eventually followed after him. Bidding good-bye to his friends, Ignatius started his 400-mile walk sometime in July 1526.[9] Situated on the Henares river, Alcalá was justly proud of its university, founded in 1508 by Cardinal Ximénez de Cisneros;[10] by 1526 it had become a renowned center of learning and humanism. Ignatius, as was his custom, supported himself by alms and he tells of an incident when a cleric publicly ridiculed him for begging when he was neither unwell nor a cripple. In the eyes of the cleric, Ignatius was but a lazy vagrant; in his own eyes, begging was his way of manifesting his total dependence on God. Another passerby witnessed that encounter and noticed how meekly the beggar accepted the rebuke; moved by this humility the gentleman, who was the administrator of the Hospital of Our Lady of Mercy also called Antezana after its founder,[11] offered Ignatius a place to live.

the new hospital of Antezana was passing by, and feeling sorry
for him, called him over and took him to the hospital, where
he gave him a room and all he needed.

57. He spent almost a year and a half studying in Alcalá;
since he had arrived in Barcelona, where he studied for two
years, during Lent 1524, he thus arrived in Alcalá in 1526. There
he studied the dialectics of Soto, the physics of Albert, and the
Master of the Sentences. While in Alcalá he engaged in giving
the Spiritual Exercises and in explaining Christian doctrine, and
by these means he brought forth fruit for the glory of God.
Many people came to a deep knowledge of and a relish for
spiritual things and others were undergoing various trials, like
the one who desired to scourge himself but was unable to, as
if someone were holding back his hand, and other such cases.
All this gave rise to much talk in the city, especially because
of the great number of people who gathered wherever he was
explaining doctrine.

57. After the summer recess the university again opened its doors to
its students. Though Ignatius mentions three courses that he followed, still
his name does not appear on any of the known lists of students attending
the university.[12] It appears more likely that he had no set plan of study,
and thus he did not matriculate but attended whatever lectures he chose.
He says that he studied the logic of Soto,[13] the natural philosophy of Albert
the Great,[14] and the theology of Peter Lombard[15] — a strange mixture of
subjects for someone just entering the academic world. When not in the
lecture halls, Ignatius was usually in the courtyard of the Antezana Hospital,
teaching catechism to children or speaking to grown-ups about the Com-
mandments and the love of God and of neighbor, and teaching his listeners
different methods of prayer, ideas which he took from the notes he had
made at Manresa and which eventually were to become the Spiritual
Exercises.

Among the people Ignatius got to know in Alcalá there was one who
was somewhat special to him and that was Diego de Eguía.[16] Diego was
then a priest and was living with his brother Miguel, a respected printer.[17]
The Eguía brothers gave lodging to Ignatius' three companions, when they
first came from Barcelona, and were most generous in supplying him with
money and whatever else he needed for the poor. In later years Diego entered
the Society in Rome and for a time served as Ignatius' confessor.

Shortly after coming to Alcalá he got to know Don Diego de Eguía, who was then living with his brother, who had a printing business in Alcalá, and was rather well off. They gave him alms to help the poor and kept three of the pilgrim's companions in their house. Once, when he asked for alms for some needs he had, Don Diego said he had no money,, but he opened a chest containing various items and gave him bed covers of different colors and some candlesticks, and other similar things. The pilgrim wrapped them all in a sheet, put them on his shoulder, and went out to assist the poor.

58. As it was already said, rumors began flying throughout that region about the things happening in Alcalá; some in-

---

58-59. Because of the number of children and women who gathered to listen to Ignatius' instructions—a sight somewhat unusual in Alcalá—stories began to be spread about him, his companions, and their teaching. Since they all wore the same type of tunic made of sackcloth, they unwillingly gave the appearance of being a special group. And since they were neither priests nor religious, but laypersons involved in street preaching, some observers undoubtedly viewed them as part of a "reform movement," perhaps even influenced by the teaching of Martin Luther. Others thought they were *alumbrados*, that is, members of a Spanish religious movement that claimed direct illumination of the Holy Spirit and considered themselves exempt from the usual means of sanctification proposed by the Church. Ignatius and his group thus came under suspicion and news of their novel activity reached the Inquisition in Toledo.

Two inquisitors came to Alcalá,[18] and together with the archbishop's representative, Juan Rodríguez de Figueroa,[19] they formed the inquisitorial board. They met at the episcopal residence on November 19, 1526, and summoning four witnesses,[20] they questioned them about the manner of life Ignatius and his companions lived and what they taught. The result was that they found nothing wrong with the group's way of life nor was there anything erroneous in their teaching. Since none of the witnesses said anything negative about Ignatius, the board felt no need to summon him. The inquisitors then returned to Toledo and left it to Figueroa to inform Ignatius of their decision. This he did on November 21. Since the board had found their life and teaching blameless, they were permitted to continue as they had been doing; however, since they did not belong to any Order and since the tunics they wore resembled a religious habit, they were

dividuals said one thing while others said something else. This matter reached the Inquisition in Toledo and when the inquisitors came to Alcalá the pilgrim was warned by their host, who told him that they were calling them "sack wearers," and "enlightened ones" I believe, and that they were going to make mincemeat of them. They immediately began an examination and investigation into their lives but in the end they returned to Toledo without summoning them, though they had come with that purpose in mind. They left the trial to the vicar Figueroa, who is now with the emperor. Several days later the vicar summoned them and informed them that an investigation and examination had been made into their lives by the inquisitors and that no error was found in their teaching nor in their living habits, and thus they could continue doing what they were doing, and without any restrictions. But since they were not members of a religious Order, it did not seem proper for all of them to go about wearing a habit. It would be better, so he ordered, if two of them, here he pointed to the pilgrim and to Arteaga, were to dye their clothes black, and the other two, Calixto and Cáceres, to dye theirs a light brown. Juanico, who was a Frenchman, could remain as he was.

59. The pilgrim said that they would do as they were

to give them up and wear the customary clothing of clerics or laymen. Figueroa must have mitigated this portion of the board's decision for rather than insisting that they get new clothing, he thought it sufficient if they merely dyed their clothes different colors so as not to appear as a group set apart. The Juanico[21] that Ignatius here mentions was a young Frenchman whom he met at the Antezana Hospital.

Though the inquisitors had exonerated his group, Ignatius still wondered how beneficial such investigations actually were. Priests in the parishes could still refuse to permit them to receive weekly Communion. Ignatius tells how one of his companions had recently been refused Communion and that he himself received similar treatment. Before departing, Ignatius sought assurance that there was nothing wrong in his actions nor error in his teaching. Figueroa replied that if there were heresy in Ignatius' teaching the inquisitors would certainly have discovered it and that they would have ordered. "But," he added, "I do not know how beneficial such investigations are. The other day a priest refused to give the Sacrament to one of us because he receives Communion every week, and they have made difficulties for me. We would like to know whether they have found any heresy in us." Figueroa answered: "No; if they had, they would have burned you." "They would have likewise burned you," the pilgrim retorted, "if they found heresy in you." They dyed their clothes as they had been ordered to do, and about two or three weeks later, Figueroa ordered the pilgrim to wear shoes and not go about barefoot. He obeyed quite peacefully, as he always did in such matters when commanded to do so.

Four months later, Figueroa himself again investigated them. In addition to the usual charges, I believe it also came about because a married woman of some prominence, who had a special interest in the pilgrim, came to the hospital one morning, at dawn, and in order not to be recognized wore a veil, as is the custom in Alcalá de Henares. When she entered the hospital, she removed her veil and went to the pilgrim's room. But they did nothing to them at that time, nor did they summon them after the investigation, nor did they say anything to them.

sentenced him to be burned. Ignatius knew that the Inquisition was no respecter of persons and so he retorted that even if heresy were found in Figueroa's teaching, he too would suffer the same penalty. The tunics were dyed, and within a few weeks Figueroa asked Ignatius not to go about barefoot, but to wear shoes. He did not want Ignatius to have anything in his manner of dress that could be interpreted as his being a monk or a religious.

On March 6, 1527, Figueroa initiated another investigation into Ignatius' teaching, but this was done on his own authority. Ignatius surmised that more denunciations must have been brought against him, and perhaps the fact that a prominent lady had once come to visit him, veiled and at a very early hour, added to these suspicions. Figueroa summoned three witnesses, but from these he heard only praise for Ignatius and found nothing wrong in his teaching.

60. Another four months later—he was now living in a small building outside the hospital—a policeman one day came to his door and calling out to him said: "Come with me for a little while!" He put him in jail and said: "You are not to leave this place until you are ordered otherwise." It was then summer and since he was not all that confined there, many people came to visit him, and he did the same there as when he was free; he gave instructions in doctrine and gave the Exercises. Though many lawyers and attorneys offered him their services, he refused them. He especially remembers Doña Teresa de Cárdenas, who sent someone to visit him and many times offered to have him released, but he wanted nothing, always saying: "He, for whose love I have come here, will set me free if His will is served thereby."

60-61. Ignatius lived in relative peace for another four months, but then in the middle of Holy Week—either Holy Thursday or Good Friday (April 18 or 19)—he was unexpectedly taken to jail without knowing the reason. It seems that his freedom was not overly restricted for friends came to visit and he continued to give instructions and lead others through the Exercises. Among his friends were lawyers who offered to represent him, but he preferred to depend on God. He especially remembered the kindness of Doña Teresa Enríquez de Cárdenas,[22] who wanted to use her influence to have him released, but again Ignatius chose to remain there until God saw fit to release him.

It was after seventeen days of imprisonment that Ignatius finally learned what had brought him there. Figueroa and a notary arrived; this was an official visit, with the notary recording all questions and answers. Of the many questions asked on that occasion, Ignatius records only two. The question about Saturday was the vicar's indirect way of asking whether Ignatius was a Jewish convert. In Spain, at that time, many Jews underwent conversion, and though they externally acted as Christians, they secretly practiced their old religious rites. To the vicar's question, Ignatius replied: "I spend my Saturdays in devotion to our Lady, and I have no other observances. Furthermore, in my country [Guipúzcoa] there are no Jews."[23] Figueroa then touched on the reason why Ignatius was in jail. A certain María del Vado and her daughter Luisa Velázquez, together with their servant Catalina, had suddenly disappeared from Alcalá.[24] Dr. Pedro Ciruelo,

61. He was in prison for seventeen days without anyone interrogating him, or without his knowing the reason for his being there. At the end of this time, Figueroa came to the prison and questioned him about many matters, even asking him if he encouraged others to observe Saturday. He asked if he knew two ladies in particular, who were mother and daughter, and to this he answered that he did. And if he had known anything of their departure before they had set out. He answered no, appealing to the oath he had taken. The vicar, placing his hand on his shoulder as a sign of his satisfaction, then said: "This was the reason why you were brought here." Among the many people who followed the pilgrim, there were a mother and daughter, both widows, and the daughter was very young and beautiful and both had made much progress in spiritual matters, but especially the daughter, and to such a degree that though they were noble ladies, they had gone on foot to the shrine of Veronica's veil in Jaén, alone and perhaps begging their way.

This caused much talk in Alcalá, and Dr. Ciruelo, who was somewhat responsible for them, thought that the prisoner had influenced them into going and thus he had him arrested. In response to what the vicar had said, the prisoner answered: "Would you like me to speak a bit more on this matter?" "Yes," he replied. "Then you should be aware," said the prisoner, "that both these women had many times enthusiastically spoken to

a professor at the university who acted as the ladies' protector, knowing that they had been in contact with Ignatius, presumed that he was responsible for their disappearance and consequently lodged a complaint with the vicar. The outcome was that a policeman led Ignatius to jail. Ignatius conceded that he knew the ladies, but he likewise added that, knowing of their desire to travel about to help the poor, he tried to dissuade them by showing that they could aid the poor in their own city, and that they could attend the priest as he carried Viaticum to the dying. Figueroa was genuinely satisfied with Ignatius' explanation, but the prisoner had to remain there until the ladies returned home to corroborate his story.

him about their desire to go through the world serving the poor in one or another hospital. I have always tried to steer them away from that plan because the daughter was so young, so attractive, and so on. I told them that whenever they wanted to visit the poor, they could do so right here in Alcalá, and they can also accompany the Most Blessed Sacrament." When this conversation ended, Figueroa left with his notary, who had written everything down.

62. At that time Calixto was in Segovia, and hearing of his imprisonment, he came at once, though he had only recently

62-63. During the period when Ignatius was waiting for the devout ladies to return, Calixto, recovering from a grave illness in Segovia, heard of Ignatius' imprisonment and came to Alcalá to join him in jail, but his already poor health only further deteriorated and Ignatius arranged to have him released.

The ladies finally returned and presented themselves to Figueroa.[25] They explained that they had made a pilgrimage to Jaén in southern Spain to visit the shrine of the Holy Face. Then they went to Guadalupe to pray before a miraculous statue of our Lady.[26] They also confessed that their pilgrimage was entirely their own doing and that Ignatius had no part in their going. Figueroa's harsh sentence was read to Ignatius by the notary on June 1. He was free but he and his companions were to dress as the other students did and were forbidden to speak on matters of the faith until they had pursued further studies.[27] Ignatius acknowledged that of his little group, he had the most education, but he likewise admitted that what he had was indeed very little. Since Figueroa's decision brought an end to his apostolate in Alcalá, Ignatius began to think of his future. Paramount in his thinking was his earnest desire to help souls, and with that in mind he determined to visit the Archbishop of Toledo, Alonso de Fonseca,[28] who was then at the royal court in Valladolid.

Ignatius left Alcalá in late June and had his conversation with the archbishop in early July. Now that Ignatius was in Valladolid, outside the archdiocese of Toledo, he told the archbishop that though he was no longer bound by the decision that Figueroa had passed in the archbishop's name, nevertheless, because of his goodwill he would still do whatever the archbishop should command after he had heard Ignatius' narration of the events of the past several months. When the archbishop heard the story he was impressed by Ignatius' sincerity, and sensing his genuine desire to help others

recovered from a serious illness, and desired to be in jail with him. But the pilgrim told him that it would be better for him to go and present himself to the vicar, who treated him kindly and said that he would give the order for him to be imprisoned, for he too should remain there until the women returned to confirm the prisoner's story. Calixto spent several days in jail, but when the pilgrim saw that it was harming his bodily health — since he was not yet fully recovered — he got him released through the services of a physician who was a good friend of his.

Forty-two days had passed from the day the pilgrim went to prison to the day he was released. At the end of that period the two devout ladies returned and the notary went to the prison to read him his sentence. He was free, but they were to dress as did the other students and they were not to speak on matters of faith for the next four years until they had pursued further studies for at present they were not sufficiently educated. It was the pilgrim, to tell the truth, who knew the most, but he had no solid foundation, and this was the first thing he usually mentioned when anyone examined him.

63. As a result of this decision he became a bit doubtful as to what he ought to do. It seemed to him that the door was now being closed on his helping souls, since they gave him no reason other than the fact that he had no formal studies. In the end he decided to go to Archbishop Fonseca of Toledo, and put his case in his hands.

He left Alcalá and met the archbishop in Valladolid. He faithfully narrated what happened and said that though he was no longer under the archbishop's jurisdiction, nor was he obliged to follow his decision, nevertheless, he would do whatever the

and to attend the University of Salamanca to pursue further his studies, the archbishop acquiesced. He told Ignatius that he had many friends in Salamanca and that he had founded the College of Saint James at the university for poor students, and all this he was willing to offer him.

archbishop commanded. He spoke to him in the same familiar manner that he used with everyone. The archbishop listened attentively and, realizing that he wanted to go to Salamanca said that he had friends in Salamanca as well as a college, and offered all this to him. As he was leaving, the archbishop gave him four *escudos*.

Chapter 7

Salamanca: On Trial
(Mid-July–Mid-September 1527)

64. After his arrival in Salamanca and while he was praying in a church, a devout lady recognized him as being one of the group, for his four companions had already been there several days. She asked him his name and then took him to the place where the companions were staying. When they passed sentence in Alcalá that they were to dress as students, the pilgrim said: "When you ordered us to dye our clothes, that we did. But

64-65. While Ignatius was on his way to visit the Archbishop of Toledo in Valladolid, his four companions left Alcalá for Salamanca. After his visit with the Spanish prelate, Ignatius walked the seventy miles to be with his friends again. Salamanca was the home of Spain's greatest university, as famous as those of Oxford and Paris. Shortly after his arrival in mid-July 1527, Ignatius was recognized by the clerical student dress he was wearing. In Alcalá he and his companions were ordered to dress like the other students, but since the students of Salamanca wore a style of dress different from that of the students in Alcalá, Ignatius and his companions unwillingly stood out from among the others. A certain woman who had come to know Ignatius' group,[1] seeing that Ignatius was wearing similar garb, surmised that he too was one of them; she approached him and took him to where his friends were staying.

Since Salamanca was outside the jurisdiction of the Archbishop of Toledo the sentence passed on him in Alcalá was without force there, so Ignatius immediately set about his apostolate of gathering children for instruction and speaking to adults about God and prayer. This new and unheard-of activity was soon brought to the attention of the Dominican friars of San Esteban, a priory known as a center of learning and as the bulwark of orthodoxy in the city. Most of its friars were professors at the university.

Following his custom of weekly confession, Ignatius visited the church

now we are not able to do what you ask since we do not have the resources to purchase new ones." Hence the vicar himself provided them with caps, clothing, and other student apparel, and thus dressed, they left Alcalá.

In Salamanca he went to confession to a friar of Saint Dominic in the church of San Esteban. One day, some ten or twelve days after his arrival, his confessor said to him: "The Fathers here in the house would like to speak with you." "In the name of God," he answered. The confessor then said: "It would be good if you would come and dine with us on Sunday, but I

---

of San Esteban. There is nothing strange in his choice of a Dominican for his confessor; he had one while in Manresa and for a time he resided in the Dominican monastery there. On his subsequent visit to his confessor — about two weeks after coming to the city — the priest told Ignatius that the friars in his community were interested in him and that he was invited to dine with them on the following Sunday. The confessor's warning that the friars would grill him on his activities did not deter him from accepting the invitation. The following day Ignatius and Calixto had dinner with the friars and afterwards the subprior, Father Nicolás de Santo Tomás,[2] together with two other friars, one of them being Ignatius' confessor, took their guests to a chapel. The subprior initiated the discussion by telling Ignatius of the good reports he had heard about them, but for the present he would like a few more details. His first question was on their educational background, and Ignatius here admitted, as he had done in Alcalá, that his theological training was but a few disconnected lectures. The second question was on the subject matter of their preaching. Ignatius gently corrected the subprior in saying that they did not preach, that is, they did not give formal discourses but rather spoke familiarly with those who came to listen. Theirs was more of a chat than a sermon. And as for the content, they spoke about virtue and sin. The subprior then came to the heart of his interrogation: If Ignatius was instructing others about virtue and sin, and since he was not educated in that area, as he himself acknowledged, then the knowledge he had must have come to him by the direct illumination of the Holy Spirit. Ignatius immediately saw the corner into which the subprior was trying to force him. If he said his knowledge came from the Holy Spirit, he would be saying that he was an *alumbrado*, and since these "enlightened ones" had been condemned by the Inquisition he would be condemning himself. Though not trained in the schools Ignatius learned

want to tell you in advance that they will want to know many things about you." So on Sunday he came with Calixto, and after dinner the subprior — the prior was absent — together with the confessor and, I believe, another friar, went with them to a chapel. With all graciousness the subprior began to speak of the good reports they received about their life and habits, and how they went about preaching like apostles, but they would now like to have more details on these matters. Thus he began by asking what studies had they done. The pilgrim answered: "Of all of us, I have studied the most," and then went on to give a clear account of the little he had studied, and how limited that training was.

65. "Then, about what do you preach?" The pilgrim said: "We do not preach, we speak to a few in a friendly manner about the things of God, just as one does after dinner with those who invite us." "But," the friar asked, "of what godly things do you speak? That is precisely what we would like to know." The pilgrim answered: "Sometimes we speak about one virtue, then another, always with praise; sometimes we speak about one vice, then another, always condemning it." "You have had no education," the friar spoke out, "and you talk about virtue and vice? No one can speak of these except

much from his various confessors, from the spiritual people with whom he spoke, from his reading, as well as from his own personal ordeal with scruples.

Ignatius wisely declined to continue the conversation, but the subprior insisted, being desirous of discovering whether Ignatius held opinions similar to those of Desiderius Erasmus,[3] or to those of the Lutherans, whose teachings had penetrated Spain. The friars at San Esteban were especially interested in Erasmus at this time because a conference of theologians was then meeting in Valladolid, having been convened by the Inquisitor General, Alonso Manrique, Archbishop of Seville.[4] The purpose of the conference was to discuss twenty-one propositions taken from Erasmus' works and to judge whether they were consonant with Catholic teaching or whether they were heretical. Because of this "Erasmus fever" in the air, the subprior pressed hard on Ignatius to reveal himself.

in either of two ways: either because of having been educated, or by the Holy Spirit. Since you have had no education, then it is by the Holy Spirit." The pilgrim was now on his guard for this way of arguing did not seem good to him. After a bit of silence he said there was no further need to discuss these matters. The friar pressed on: "With so many errors now deceiving the world, as those of Erasmus and of many others, you are unwilling to explain what you mean?"

66. The pilgrim replied: "Father, I will say nothing more than what I have said, except in the presence of my superiors who can oblige me to do so." Before this the friar had asked why Calixto came dressed as he did. He wore a short coat with a large hat on his head, a staff in his hand and boots halfway up his legs. Since he was very tall, all this made him look quite ridiculous. The pilgrim told him the story of how they had been imprisoned in Alcalá and that they had been ordered to wear the clothes that students wore, and since it was very hot his companion had given his long student's gown to a poor cleric. Here the friar, making it clear that this did not please

---

66-67. Since the subprior was not his ecclesiastical superior, Ignatius refused to continue the discussion. But now that the subprior's suspicions had been aroused, he asked Ignatius and Calixto to remain at the monastery. Their stay lasted three days, during which time the subprior took Ignatius' case to the diocesan court judges to initiate proceedings against him, but never was Ignatius informed that the friars were bringing him to trial. At the end of three days Ignatius and Calixto were taken to a prison and their cell, though not a dungeon and not with common criminals, was musty, filthy, and rodent infested.[5] The chain binding their legs was about a yard long, and since they were without mats for sleeping and had rodents wandering freely about the cell, it is no wonder that their first night was sleepless.

Martin Frías,[6] vicar-general of the Bishop of Salamanca, called by the title bachelor to distinguish him from another judge with the same name, questioned both prisoners. Learning where their companions Arteaga and Cáceres were lodging, Frías sent prison attendants to arrest them as well, but these two were placed in an underground cell. Only Juanico remained free, perhaps because of his youth. Ignatius mentions, without giving any

him, mumbled between his teeth, "Charity begins at home."

But returning to the story, the subprior, not being able to get another word out of the pilgrim except that one, said: "Remain here; we will easily get you to tell all." All the friars then departed in some haste. First the pilgrim asked if they wanted them to wait in that chapel, or wherever else they would want them to wait. The subprior answered that they were to remain in the chapel. The friars then locked all the doors and went, it seems, to discuss the matter with the judges. The two of them stayed at the monastery for three days, eating in the refectory with the monks, without anything being said to them about a trial. Their room was almost always full of friars who came to see them, and the pilgrim always spoke about the things that he usually talked about. As a consequence a division arose among the monks, for many showed that their sympathy was with them.

67. At the end of three days a notary came and led them to prison. They were not put underground with the criminals, but in an upper room which, because it was old and unused, contained a lot of rubbish. They were bound together by one and the same chain, each by his foot; the chain was attached to a post in the middle of the room and was about ten to thirteen palms long, and every time one wanted to do something, the other had to go with him. All that night they remained awake. The following day, when the news spread in the city that they were in prison, their friends sent them mats for sleeping and an abundant supply of whatever else they needed. Many kept on coming to see them and the pilgrim continued in his practice of speaking about God, and so forth.

time reference, that Juanico became a friar; other sources indicate that he entered the Franciscans.[7] With this preliminary interrogation over, Frías left the prison, taking with him Ignatius' copy of the Exercises. There is no way of knowing how developed the Exercises were at this time — were they already in a first-draft stage, or were they just a collection of notes that would eventually become the Spiritual Exercises?

Bachelor Frías came to question them individually, and the pilgrim gave him all his notes, which were the Exercises, for examination. Asked if they had companions, they said they did and told where they were. Following the bachelor's order, they immediately went there and brought Cáceres and Arteaga to the prison, but left Juanico behind, who later became a friar. They did not place them in the upper room with the other two, but below, where the ordinary prisoners were kept. Here also he did not want to have any lawyer or attorney.

68. Several days later he was summoned before four judges: the Doctors were Sanctisidoro, Paravinhas, and Frías, and the fourth was Bachelor Frías, all of whom had already seen the Exercises. They now questioned him about many things, not only about the Exercises, but in theology, for example, on the Trinity and the Blessed Sacrament, and how he understood these

68. After the four judges appointed to hear the case had read through the Exercises, they called Ignatius to appear before them. Three were Doctors of Law, and the fourth was Bachelor Frías. Of the three doctors whose names Ignatius records, scholars think that the Sanctisidoro may have been Fernando Rodríguez de San Isidoro, and that Frías was probably Francisco de Frías. Neither the name Paravinhas, nor one similar to it appears in the Salamanca diocesan records; a copyist may have made an unwitting orthographic change in the name.[8] Ignatius successfully answered all the questions asked him, whether on the Trinity or the Eucharist, and so thorough was his explanation of the First Commandment that the judges did not want to sit through the same lengthy exposition for the other nine. On one topic, however, the judges showed great tenacity. In the Exercises, in the part entitled "General Examen of Conscience," Ignatius speaks of sins of thought and gives guidelines on how to determine when these thoughts are mortally or venially sinful. What perplexed the learned judges was that someone as theologically uneducated as Ignatius was capable of determining when a thought is a mortal or a venial sin. Having himself been the victim of scruples, Ignatius tried his utmost to teach his listeners how to distinguish between such sinful thoughts so that they might not have to endure the same torment that he had gone through. Unable to condemn any point in Ignatius' explanation the judges brought the interrogation to a close.

articles of faith. He first gave an introduction, but being ordered by the judges, he spoke in such a way that they had no reason whatever to censure him. Bachelor Frías, who always pressed him more than the others, also asked a question in canon law. Being obliged to answer every question, he always prefaced his remarks saying that he did not know what the learned doctors held on these points. Then they ordered him to explain the First Commandment as he usually explained it. This he started to do, and did it in so great detail, saying so many things about the First Commandment, that they no longer had any desire to ask anything more of him. Previously, when they were discussing the Exercises, they showed great insistence on a single point, which is at the beginning of the Exercises: When is a thought a venial sin, and when is it a mortal sin? Their problem was that he, though uneducated, was determining that question. He responded: "Decide whether what I say is true or not; if it is not true, condemn it." In the end they left without condemning anything.

69. Among the many who came to see him in prison was Don Francisco de Mendoza, who is now Cardinal of Burgos, and on that occasion he came with Bachelor Frías. Speaking as a friend would, he asked how he was getting along in prison and whether being there weighed heavily upon him. He replied: "As my answer I will give the same that I today gave a lady

---

69. The one visitor that Ignatius mentions by name was Don Francisco de Mendoza.[9] At the time of his visit he was only nineteen and was teaching Greek at the University of Salamanca. Ignatius' answer to him should not be read as if he rejected Mendoza's manifestation of compassion, but as Ignatius seeing his days of confinement as days of praise to God, and that he was willing to bear even greater suffering for the love of God.

Since there was a jailbreak among the inmates in the dungeon area and since Arteaga and Cáceres refused to escape with the others, the prison officials were greatly moved by their innate goodness and honesty. In recognition of Arteaga's and Caceres' integrity, Ignatius and his companions were moved to a nearby residence and were kept under house arrest.

who, when seeing me imprisoned, spoke words of compassion. I told her: 'By this you show that you do not desire to be taken prisoner for the love of God. Does imprisonment appear to be so great an evil to you? Then I will tell you that there are not enough fetters and chains in Salamanca that I would not desire more for the love of God.' "

At this time it happened that all the prisoners made their escape, but the two companions who were with them did not flee. When they were found the next morning, all alone with doors wide open, everyone was deeply edified, and this caused much talk in the city. Because of this they put all of them in a nearby mansion as their prison.

70. After twenty-two days of imprisonment they were summoned to hear their sentence. No error was discovered either in their life-style or in their teaching; therefore they could continue as they had been doing, teaching doctrine and speaking about the things of God as long as they did not determine "This is a mortal sin" or "This is a venial sin," until they had completed four years of study. When the sentence was read, the judges manifested great kindness, since they wanted them to agree to the sentence. The pilgrim said that he would fulfill all that the sentence orders, but that he does not agree with it for though not condemning him on any single point, they

---

70. As in his previous encounters with ecclesiastical courts, no error was found in Ignatius' teaching. Unlike the Alcalá sentence, Ignatius and his companions were permitted to continue their apostolate, but with the single restriction of not determining, until they had completed four years of formal theological training, whether a thought is mortally or venially sinful.

Ignatius made known his willingness to obey the sentence, but he did mention that he did not agree with it. Since he was accused of no error whatever, and since it was imperative in Ignatius' eyes to teach the faithful how to distinguish between mortal and venial sins in order to avoid scruples and to make their confessions more fruitful, he interpreted this sentence as forcibly silencing him in the very area where he could best help others. The four companions, now released from prison, had to think of their future.

were forcing his mouth closed so as to keep him from helping others in the way that he could. Though Doctor Frías strongly urged them to agree, and gave signs that he was sympathetic, the pilgrim said nothing else except that as long as he remained within the jurisdiction of Salamanca he would do as had been ordered.

Then and there they were released from prison and he began to commend the matter to God and to think of what he should do. He found great difficulty in staying in Salamanca because this prohibition on determining which are mortal and which are venial sins closed the door on his helping souls.

71. Thus he decided on going to Paris to study. In Barcelona, when the pilgrim was deliberating whether he should study and for how many years, his main concern was whether, after his studies, he should enter religion or continue going about the world. With the thought of entering religion, he also thought of entering a congregation that was lax and unreformed so that he could suffer the more in it. He thought that God would perhaps help it, for God granted him a deep assurance that he could successfully endure all the insults and hurts that they might inflict upon him.

During the period of his imprisonment in Salamanca he was not without the same desire to help souls, and with that as his goal he decided to study and to win over like-minded individuals and keep those he had. Once he had decided on going to Paris, he arranged with the other companions to wait where they were while he went to see if he could find the means by which they also could study.

72. Many prominent individuals urgently begged him not to leave, but they could never convince him. Fifteen or twenty

71-72. A few years before, when Ignatius was in Barcelona he had wondered whether he should give himself to studies—he was in his thirties—and whether after studies he should enter a religious Order or continue as he was in the world. Because of the desire he then had of doing

days after leaving prison he set out by himself, carrying some books on a donkey. When he came to Barcelona, all who knew him tried to dissuade him from going into France because of the violent battles going on there, and they narrated many specific incidents, even telling him that they skewered Spaniards on spits. But never did he have any fear.

great penances, the thought of entering a lax Order seemed to fit his plans. Perhaps God, taking into account his penitential life, would inspire such a congregation to reform. For himself, he was certain that he was capable of enduring all the personal affronts that others could heap upon him. But after his days in Barcelona, he was convinced that he was called by God to help others, and during his incarceration in Salamanca this desire to help others was always foremost in his thoughts. If he were now to join a religious Order it would have been the Conventual Franciscans because of their work among the faithful rather than the more cloistered Observants.[10] But he first had to begin his studies if he wanted to be of help to others and so Ignatius decided on going to the University of Paris. He told his companions that he would go on ahead and would find the money for them to follow him.

Hearing of Ignatius' desire to leave Salamanca, his friends tried to talk him out of his plans, but two or three weeks after his release from prison he set out, in mid-September, with a donkey carrying his books. The total time he spent in Salamanca was about two months, and he never got the chance to matriculate at Archbishop Fonseca's college for poor students. During his time in Salamanca someone gave him books that would be of use to him in his studies, and someone else supplied him with a donkey to make the trip easier. When Ignatius came to Barcelona his friends there also tried to talk him out of traveling to France, going to such extremes as to narrate horror stories of what the French were doing to Spaniards when they were caught. With complete confidence in God Ignatius resolutely set his face toward Paris and looked to the future.

Chapter 8

Paris: University Studies
and First Companions

(February 2, 1528–April 1535)

73. Alone and on foot he set out for Paris and arrived there in the month of February, more or less; I think it was in the year 1528 or 1527. He found lodging in a house with several

73. After a good month's walk of almost 700 miles, and in the cold of winter, Ignatius finally arrived in the City of Light, his home for the next six years. He left no record of the cities he visited, nor of any incident along the way. Because of the time of year his route to Paris must have been the most direct,[1] bringing him there on February 2, 1528.[2] He passed through Porte Saint-Jacques, and using the few French words he had learned, he discovered where the Spaniards made their home in that great city. As he was leaving Barcelona his friends forced upon him a draft of twenty-five *escudos*, redeemable in Paris, and meant to supply him with the funds he would need to get settled and begin studies. When he redeemed the draft he gave the money to a compatriot of his for safekeeping; because he himself was honest, Ignatius thought everyone else was honest.

Classes were in session and Ignatius registered at Collège de Montaigu but learned, after an entrance exam, that his study of Latin grammar in Barcelona must have been done in too hurried a fashion because his background was still insufficient for advanced work. So he decided to repeat these courses, attending classes with boys in their early teens and even younger, and when he successfully passed one stage he advanced to another, following the established program then in force in Paris. Montaigu[3] was one of the more than fifty colleges making up the University of Paris, and one of the schools frequented by the Spanish and Portuguese. When Easter came — April 12 that year — he found that the trust he had placed in his fellow Spaniard was indeed misplaced for the latter had spent the money on himself leaving Ignatius without a cent. He now had no other alterna-

Spaniards and began studying humanities at Montaigu. The reason why he did this was because they had made him advance through his studies with so great haste that he found that he was without a good foundation. He went to class with young lads and made progress according to the prescribed curriculum of Paris.

As soon as he arrived in Paris a shopkeeper gave him twenty-five *escudos* on a draft from Barcelona, and these he gave to one of the Spaniards where he was staying for safekeeping, but the Spaniard squandered them in a very short time and had no way of repaying him. When Lent was over, the pilgrim had no money because of what he had spent as well as for the above-mentioned reason, and thus he was forced to go begging and even had to leave the house where he was staying.

74. He was accepted at the Hospital Saint-Jacques, beyond the church of the Innocents. This was especially inconvenient

---

tive but to beg his bread, and since he was unable to pay for his room he began searching for a place that would take him in as a nonpaying guest.

74-75. Ignatius found a room at the Hospital Saint-Jacques,[4] a hospice for pilgrims on their way to the shrine of Santiago de Compostela. Living at the hospital proved to be a great disadvantage to Ignatius. Although it was more than a mile walk to Montaigu, it was not the walking that distressed the lame Ignatius, but the fact that the horarium at the hospital conflicted with that of the college. The hospital opened its doors only when the sun rose and closed them early with the sound of the evening Angelus. Ignatius' first class, on the other hand, was at 5 a.m., and his last at 7 p.m., which meant missing both these classes. Many such absences, together with the time spent in begging, had their effect on his classwork, and since his chief purpose for being in Paris was to study, he judged that he could not long continue at the hospital but would have to seek another arrangement. It might be possible, he thought, to secure a position as servant to one of the regents, that is, one of the younger professors in one of the colleges. Such a position would not only give him his room and board and supply him with some funds to pay for his education, but it would at the same time allow him the leisure he needed for his studies. He viewed such a job as an opportunity to exercise humility, for in being obedient to the regent or to one of the students, he was being obedient to Christ and the

for his classes since the hospital was a good distance from the Collège de Montaigu, and he had to return home before the ringing of the *Ave Maria* in order to find the door open, and had to leave at daylight. As a result he could not conveniently attend his lectures. Another drawback was the fact that he had to beg alms in order to support himself.

About five years had passed since he had any stomach pain and so he began to fast and practice greater penances. Living for some time in this way, at the hospital and by begging, and seeing that he was making little progress in his studies, he started to think about what he should do. He knew that there were some who served several of the regents in the colleges and had time for their studies, so he decided to look for someone to employ him.

75. He kept mulling over this idea and found consolation in it because he imagined that his master would be Christ, and to one student he gave the name Saint Peter, and to another Saint John, and so on with each of the apostles. "When the master gives me an order I will think that it is Christ commanding me, and when someone else gives me an order I will think that it is Saint Peter commanding me." He tried his hardest to find an employer, and on one occasion he spoke to Bachelor Castro, and on another to a Carthusian friar, who was acquainted with many of the masters, and to others too but they were never able to find a job for him.

76. Not finding any solution, a Spanish friar eventually told him that it would be better for him to go each year to

apostles. He took this idea to Juan Castro,[5] who had recently received his bachelor's degree, asking him if he knew of anyone who could employ him, but neither Castro, nor a Carthusian monk, nor any of the others he had asked, were able to do anything for him.

76. Ignatius made his first begging tour to Flanders during Lent 1529. Flanders was an ideal place for such a tour, not only because it was part of the Spanish empire, but because its two centers of international commerce, Bruges and Antwerp, had a large number of wealthy Spanish mer-

Flanders, giving up two months or less, and to return with enough funds to study for an entire year. After he had commended this idea to God it seemed good to him, and following that advice each year he brought back from Flanders enough so that he could continue in some way. Once he even went to England and brought back more alms than he usually did in other years.

77. Upon his first return from Flanders he began with greater earnestness than before, to hold spiritual conversations and was giving the Exercises, almost simultaneously, to three individuals, that is, to Peralta, to Bachelor Castro, who was at the Sorbonne, and to Amador, a Basque who was at Sainte-Barbe. These men underwent great changes and they promptly gave all that they had to the poor, even their books, and took up begging alms in Paris. They went to live in the Hospital

chants. It was to these merchants that Ignatius had gone. On his first visit to Bruges, Ignatius met and dined with the celebrated Spanish humanist, Juan Luís Vives,[6] who had once been private secretary to the English Queen, Catherine of Aragon, and was relieved of that position when he refused to go along with Henry VIII's desire to divorce her. The trip to Flanders was a success and since Ignatius' life-style was modest and simple, what he collected was sufficient to support him for a full year and to help other poor students as well. His second and third trips to Flanders were during the months of August and September 1530 and 1531. He again visited his merchant friends, but rather than having him return each year many of them agreed to send their contributions in the future directly to Ignatius in Paris. After the Flanders visit in 1531, perhaps encouraged to do so by Vives, Ignatius went over to London, and from the Spanish merchants living in the English capital he collected more funds that he usually collected after weeks in Flanders.

77-78. Since his visit to Flanders had proven worthwhile, Ignatius left the inconveniently located Hospital Saint-Jacques and found a room somewhere in the university district itself, and began giving the Exercises to three of his acquaintances. Juan Castro[7] was then teaching at the Sorbonne, Pedro de Peralta[8] was living at Montaigu and completing his master's degree, and Amador de Elduayen,[9] a Guipúzcoan as was Ignatius, was a student at Collège de Sainte-Barbe, located directly across from Montaigu.

Saint-Jacques, where the pilgrim once stayed and whence he left for the reasons given above. This caused a great tumult in the university for the first two were distinguished and famous personages. Without wasting any time the Spanish students entered into heated argument with the two masters, but unable to get them to return to the university, either by persuasion or reason, a large group of the students, one day, with arms in their hands, went and hauled their masters from the hospital.

78. Upon bringing the masters back to the university they all agreed on the following: after the masters had completed their courses they could then proceed with their plans. Bachelor

As a result of the meditations that Ignatius had given these young men, the three of them had decided to relinquish their academic careers, give away whatever belongings they possessed, even to sacrificing their books, and enter upon a life of poverty, living in the hospital where Ignatius had lived and begging their food in the Paris streets. Their decision seems to have come about while Ignatius was absent from Paris on a mission of charity to Rouen (see #79). Though Castro and Peralta had given up their teaching positions, the students would not go along with this desire of theirs; the students considered this change in them a temporary derangement. When they were unable to bring them back to the university by peaceable means, the students resorted to force and physically dragged them back, and would not set them free until both masters had agreed to complete the courses they had begun.

Since Castro and Peralta had become attached to Ignatius, the Spanish students held Ignatius responsible for their madness. Diogo de Gouvea,[10] the principal at Sainte-Barbe, was likewise angered with Ignatius since his student, Amador, had fallen under the latter's influence. Gouvea's wrath reached such a peak that he swore that if Ignatius were ever to visit Sainte-Barbe he would have him undergo the shameful punishment of a public flogging for having seduced Amador from his studies. Ignatius refers to him as "our master," the usual title the students gave to their professors who had received the doctorate degree. Gouvea's anger was short-lived for within weeks of this threat Ignatius moved from Montaigu to Sainte-Barbe.

In time both Castro and Peralta returned to Spain and when Ignatius was narrating these events to Father Gonçalves da Câmara, Castro was prior of the Charterhouse of Porta Coeli in Valencia, and Peralta was a famous preacher in Toledo's cathedral.

Castro later went to Spain, was a preacher in Burgos for a time, and then became a Carthusian friar in Valencia. Peralta set out on foot as a pilgrim for Jerusalem. He was detained in Italy by a captain, a relative of his, who saw to it that he was brought before the pope and that he was commanded to return to Spain. These things happened, not immediately, but some years later.

In Paris a slander campaign began against the pilgrim, especially among the Spaniards. Our Master de Gouvea said that he [the pilgrim] had turned Amador, who was a member of his college, into a madman, and was determined, so he said, that the first time he [the pilgrim] set foot in Sainte-Barbe, he would give him a public whipping in the hall for being a seducer of students.

79. The Spaniard, with whom he had stayed in the beginning and who squandered his money without repaying it, left for Spain by way of Rouen. While waiting for passage in

79. After he had given the Exercises to Castro, Peralta, and Amador, Ignatius received a letter from the Spaniard who had squandered Ignatius' money, informing him that he was in Rouen on his way to Spain but had fallen ill. The Spaniard undoubtedly realized that his letter would touch Ignatius and that he would come to him without being asked. Setting aside the fact that the man had once cheated him, Ignatius made up his mind to go and help him in any way he could. He also thought he might be able to convert the man to a new way of life, and with the man's conversion in mind Ignatius decided to make the journey into a penance. Not only would he walk that distance barefoot, but he would do it without food and drink. Such a harsh penance would cause fear in anyone, but Ignatius would not permit it to sway his thinking, and so he went to the nearby Dominican church on Rue Saint-Jacques, praying that God would grant him the strength to carry out what he had determined to do. He set out for Rouen sometime in September, and though he started his journey filled with fear, it finally left him after he had passed Argenteuil, which was only six miles from Paris and was famous in the Middle Ages for possessing one of Christ's robes.[11] Walking more than half that distance on the first day — the remainder of the trip was more difficult because of his hunger and thirst — Ignatius covered the seventy-six miles in three days. He found the sick Spaniard and comforted him not only with words, but cared for

Rouen, he fell ill. Learning from a letter of his that he was quite sick, the pilgrim had the desire to go visit and assist him. At the same time he thought that through such a meeting he could win him over so that he would leave the world and devote himself totally to the service of God.

In order to accomplish his purpose he covered the twenty-eight leagues from Paris to Rouen by walking barefoot, and without eating and drinking. While praying over this proposal he found that he became filled with fright and, finally, he went to the church of Saint Dominic and there determined to go ahead with his plans, for his great fear that he was tempting God had now left him.

The following day, the morning of his departure, he woke up very early and as he was about to get dressed so great a dread took hold of him that it was almost as if he were unable to dress himself. Still feeling this aversion he left the house and the city before full daylight. That fear stayed with him and lasted until Argenteuil, which is a fortified town three leagues from Paris on the road to Rouen and where our Lord's robe is said to be. He passed by that fortress, still suffering his spiritual anguish, but as he climbed a hill that anguish began to disappear. Great consolation and spiritual strength took its place and with so much joy that he began to shout over the fields and speak aloud to God, and so forth. He spent that night with a poor beggar in a hospital, having walked fourteen leagues that day. The following night he spent in a barn, and on the third day he reached Rouen–all this time eating and drinking nothing, and barefoot just as he had planned. In Rouen he consoled the sick man and helped him board a ship going to Spain,

him, and when a ship was about to sail for Spain he helped him aboard and probably helped defray the man's passage. In return for all this Ignatius only asked him to deliver letters to his three friends in Salamanca. The fact that Ignatius had no letter for Juanico indicates that somewhere between Ignatius' departure from Salamanca (September 1527) and the present (September 1529), Juanico had become a Franciscan.

and gave him letters addressed to his companions in Salamanca, namely, to Calixto, Cáceres, and Arteaga.

80. To avoid saying anything more about these companions, this is what happened to them.

The pilgrim frequently wrote to them from Paris, as they had agreed, about the slight chance there was of his bringing them to Paris to study. But he wrote a letter to Doña Leonor Mascarenhas, asking her to assist Calixto by writing a letter to the court of the King of Portugal so that he could be given one of the scholarships that the king had established in Paris. Doña Leonor gave the letter to Calixto, with a mule for the journey and money for expenses. Calixto went to the Portuguese king's court, but in the end he did not come to Paris. When he returned to Spain he went to "the emperor's India," with a certain spiritually inclined lady. He later returned to Spain, and again went to the same India and then came back to Spain a wealthy man, astonishing all who had previously known him in Salamanca.

80. Ignatius interrupts the natural flow of his narrative to tell us what eventually happened to his three companions. He kept in touch with them, but because he had barely enough resources to sustain himself he could not, at that time, ask the three of them to come to Paris. In the case of Calixto there was some hope. Calixto may have been of Portuguese stock since Ignatius asked Doña Leonor Mascarenhas[12] to write to the Portuguese king requesting that one of the scholarships that the king had founded at Sainte-Barbe be given him. It is unknown whether a scholarship had been offered to Calixto or not; in any case, he did not go to Paris. In 1531 he went to "the emperor's India," the common name then for Mexico;[13] when he returned after his second visit, he came back a rich man and settled down in Salamanca.

As for Cáceres, Ignatius' brief statement indicates his disappointment in him. Arteaga seems to have done well for himself. He received not only worldly honors, but likewise ecclesiastical honors, for he was appointed Bishop of Chiapa in Mexico. When he arrived in Veracruz he was already sick but continued on to Mexico City where the unfortunate accident happened.[14]

Cáceres returned to Segovia, his birthplace, and began to live in such a way that he seems to have forgotten his earlier resolves.

Arteaga had been raised to a knighthood. Later, when the Society was established in Rome, he was given a bishopric in India, and wrote to the pilgrim asking that it be given to someone in the Society, but the pilgrim responded negatively to it. He was made a bishop and went to India and died there in a most strange manner: during his illness, there were two bottles of water for his refreshment; one had the water that the physician prescribed for him, the other contained water with a corrosive sublimate, a poison, and this latter was given to him by mistake and it killed him.

81. The pilgrim returned to Paris from Rouen and learned that widespread rumors had been broadcast against him because of what had happened to Castro and Peralta, and that the inquisitor had asked about him. Not wanting to wait any longer he went to the inquisitor, telling him that he had heard that he had been looking for him and that he was ready for whatever he might wish. (The inquisitor was our Master Ory, a friar of Saint Dominic.) He [the pilgrim] asked him to hurry the matter along because he intended to begin his courses in the liberal arts on the feast of Saint Remy and he would first like to have this over so that he could better attend to his studies. The inquisitor never again called him, but only told him that it was true that they had spoken about his activities, and so on.

---

81. Ignatius returned to Paris sometime in the latter part of September, when the Castro-Peralta tumult had subsided. But during his absence his name had been brought before the Inquisition[15] and inquiries had been made about him. When he did return he went directly to the Dominican monastery where Master Ory[16] resided, presented himself and requested that the investigation not be postponed since classes began on October 1. The fact that Master Ory never again summoned Ignatius signifies that the Castro-Peralta affair had completely abated.

82. Shortly after this came the feast of Saint Remy, which is the beginning of October, and he sat in on courses in the liberal arts under a teacher whose name was Master Juan Peña. He began his courses intending to keep those companions of his, who had determined to serve the Lord, and not go about looking to add others so that he could comfortably give himself to his studies.

82. Toward the end of September 1529, Ignatius matriculated at Collège de Sainte-Barbe[17] and was to begin his study of philosophy on October 1, the feast of Saint Remy. He was assigned to live with three others: Master Juan Peña,[18] who was then teaching philosophy at Sainte-Barbe and was to be Ignatius' teacher, and two students, Peter Faber,[19] a Savoyard, and Francis Xavier,[20] a Navarrese. Faber and Xavier had been in Paris since 1525, were fifteen years younger than Ignatius, and had already attained their bachelor's degrees. Ignatius' firm intention was to spend his time on his studies while keeping in contact with the friends he had made; he knew he would not have the leisure to search out more companions.

As soon as Ignatius settled into the rhythm of his lectures, he was afflicted by the same problem he had experienced in Barcelona, of spiritual thoughts invading his mind and bringing him distraction. Since he had once had this temptation and had overcome it, he surmised that the remedy used then would again work now. So he went to Master Peña and explained why he had not been doing well, and promised to be faithful in attending class and in studying. To help him catch up with the others, Master Peña asked Faber to help Ignatius by tutoring him.

During his years at Sainte-Barbe Ignatius gained four more companions. The next to join him was Simón Rodrigues,[21] a Portuguese, who had been at Sainte-Barbe since 1527 but who did not become friendly with Ignatius until October 1532. The next two were Spaniards, Diego Laínez[22] and Alfonso Salmerón.[23] Both had been students at the University of Alcalá, and because they had heard much about the Ignatius who once had been there, they decided to go to Paris and find this remarkable man. They arrived in Paris in early 1533. The last of Ignatius' first companions was Nicolas Bobadilla,[24] who came to the French capital in the fall of 1533 to continue his study of languages.

It was only in 1534, after he had six companions—all men imbued with the same vision—that Ignatius took them through the Exercises. Faber spent January in retreat, then during the spring Laínez and Salmerón followed,

As he began to attend the lectures in course the same temptations began to disturb him as those that had come when he was studying grammar in Barcelona. Whenever he was at a lecture he was unable to remain attentive because of the many spiritual thoughts that came to him. Realizing that he was, in this way, gaining little profit from the lectures, he went to his teacher and promised never to be absent but to attend the entire course as long as he was able to find bread and water to keep himself alive. Once he had made this promise all those devout thoughts, which were coming to him at the wrong time, left him and he quietly went on with his studies. During this period he was carrying on conversations with Master Peter Faber and Master Francis Xavier, both of whom he later won to God's service through the Exercises.

At this juncture in his studies no one was harassing him as previously. With reference to this, Doctor Frago once told him that he was surprised that he was quietly getting along without anyone causing him any trouble. He replied: "The reason is because I do not speak to anyone of the things of God, but when the course is over, I will return to it as usual."

then Rodrigues and Bobadilla; Xavier made the Exercises in September of that year. It may at first seem strange that of these companions Ignatius mentions only Faber and Xavier, but he recalls these not only because they were his roommates when he first went to Sainte-Barbe, but also because both had already died — Faber in Rome (1546), and Xavier off the coast of China (1552).

Ignatius' years in Paris, after the tumult caused by the change in Castro and Peralta, were calm and serene. Doctor Jerónimo Frago,[25] a professor of Scripture at the Sorbonne and a friend of Ignatius, had remarked about this in talking to him. Ignatius still intended to search out more disciples, but not during the school year. According to Divine Providence it happened that he did not have to go far in search of them; he found disciples in his roommates (Faber and Xavier), in those who had come to Paris to be with him (Laínez and Salmerón), and in those who, once they had gotten to know him, chose to walk with him (Rodrigues and Bobadilla).

83. While both of them were talking together, a friar came to ask Doctor Frago if he would find him a house, because in the house where he had a room many had died, from the plague he thought, for the plague was then beginning to spread in Paris. Doctor Frago and the pilgrim wanted to go and see the house and they took a woman with them who understood these matters and after she had gone in she confirmed that it was the plague. The pilgrim also wanted to enter and finding the sick person, he comforted him and touched his sore with his hand. After he had consoled and encouraged the man a bit, he departed alone. He began to feel pain in his hand and it seemed to him that he had the plague. This fantasy was so strong that he could not banish it until he thrust his hand into his mouth, turning it around this way and that, and said: "If you have the plague in your hand, you will also have it in your mouth." And as soon as he had done this the fantasy vanished as did the pain in his hand.

84. But when he returned to the Collège de Sainte-Barbe, where he was then living and following courses, those in the

83. The plague to which Ignatius refers is the one that began in Paris in 1531, but which did not become critical until August 1533, when institutions closed and people fled the city.[26] Since he says his visit to the house was at the time when the plague was just beginning to spread, this must have been in 1531 or early 1532. After Ignatius had visited and touched the stricken individual, his imagination began to play tricks on him and he felt certain that he had contracted the plague. On this occasion Ignatius followed his principle of *vince teipsum*, that is, by embracing something that is naturally repugnant we overcome it. Indeed, by touching the afflicted man and putting his hand into his mouth Ignatius may have manifested heroism of spirit, but was his action in accord with the virtue of prudence? Ignatius was still in the process of learning, and later in life he would not have acted as he did that day in Paris.[27]

84. At the university the philosophy course lasted three and a half years, but at the completion of the first two years the student was eligible for the bachelor's degree; after the full three and a half years, he was eligible for the licentiate degree. In January 1532, having completed his two years,

college, who knew that he had been in a house infected with the plague, ran from him and would not permit him to enter and, thus, he was forced to remain outside for a few days.

There is a custom in Paris that the students in their third year of liberal arts, in order to receive the baccalaureate degree, must "take the stone," as they say, and since this costs an *escudo*, some of the very poor students are unable to do this. The pilgrim doubted whether it would be good for him to take it. Finding

Ignatius stood as a candidate for his first degree. The students referred to this as "taking the stone." The precise meaning of this Parisian phrase has never been preserved, but it has been suggested that the expression may describe the custom in use at the University of Coimbra when a student presented himself for a degree. The candidate went before several examiners, and while the latter sat in their professorial chairs, the candidate sat on a stone in front of each examiner and answered the questions that the examiner put to him.[28] When the candidate finished with one examiner he then passed on to another, sitting on another stone, etc. To sit on the stone in the professor's presence was meant to signify the student's humility in the presence of his master. That such an examination should carry the heavy fee of an *escudo* is somewhat understandable when we realize that the fee not only covered the necessary testimonial letters, but most of it was used to defray the elaborate banquet that the graduates, by custom in medieval universities, had to provide for their professors.

What led Ignatius to hesitate about taking the degree? He does not give any hint as to the nature of his doubt, but some have proposed that since Ignatius had determined to live poorly, he considered the payment of the fee as being contrary to his resolve,[29] while others say that his doubt arose because to him taking a degree was tantamount to seeking honors,[30] and thus contrary to humility. In any case, the professor whom he approached, probably Master Peña, for some reason or other encouraged him to take the degree.

At the time when Ignatius received his bachelor's degree, he was working toward his licentiate, and successfully passed these examinations on March 13, 1533.[31] Ignatius was now ready to begin his program in theology and in October he started his theological course with the Dominicans at Saint-Jacques.

During these final months of study the pain in his stomach returned; it never was accurately diagnosed and it remained with him until his death.[32]

himself in a state of uncertainty and with no solution, he determined to place the matter in the hands of his teacher who advised him to take it and so he took it. Nonetheless, there were those who criticized him, and at least one Spaniard passed remarks about it.

About this time during his stay in Paris, his stomach began to act up, so that every two weeks he had stomach pain that lasted a good hour and brought on a fever. On one occasion the pain lasted for sixteen or seventeen hours. By this time he had already completed his liberal arts course and had studied theology for a couple of years and had gathered companions. His affliction was growing worse and he was unable to find any remedy, though he had tried many.

85. The physicians kept saying that there was nothing that could benefit him more than the air of his homeland. Further-

---

85-86. As a consequence of praying the Exercises, each of Ignatius' companions was more committed to God than before. Each now desired to be a priest and to spend his life in bringing spiritual benefit to other souls. To strengthen their companionship and to make visible their unity of heart and mind, the seven companions decided to take private vows of chastity, of poverty—to be practiced when they had completed their studies—and to go to Jerusalem to work for the conversion of the Turks. If unable to remain in the Holy Land, or if after a year's wait in Venice they were unable to go to the Holy Land, they would then go to Rome and place themselves at the disposal of the Holy Father. The date chosen for these vows was Saturday, August 15, 1534, the feast of the Assumption of our Lady.

Early that morning, shortly after sunrise and unnoticed by the Parisians, the seven companions made their way up to the Montmartre section of the city. They met at a prearranged spot and together they advanced to the chapel of Saint-Denis. The chapel was under the care of Benedictine nuns and was believed to mark the spot where Saint Denis, the first Bishop of Paris, and his companions, Saints Rusticus and Eleutherius, were martyred in the third century.[33] In the chapel's dimly lit crypt Faber, the only priest in the group—he had been ordained the previous May—celebrated the Mass. Before receiving Holy Communion, each in turn pronounced his vows as the group had planned. Ignatius was the eldest of the seven, being forty-three years old; the youngest was Salmerón, a mere nineteen.

more, his companions gave him the same advice, and they did it with some urgency. By this time they had all decided on what they would do, that is, go to Venice and Jerusalem, and spend their lives there helping souls, and if permission be not granted them to remain in Jerusalem, they would return to Rome and offer themselves to the Vicar of Christ so that he could use them wherever he judged it would be for the greater glory of God and the good of souls. They had likewise made plans to wait an entire year in Venice before sailing, and if there were no sailings to the East that year they would be free of their vow of going to Jerusalem and would go and see the pope.

In the end, the pilgrim let his companions persuade him, and also because those who were Spaniards had some business that he could settle for them. They all agreed that after he got better he was to attend to their business, and then leave for Venice and there wait for his companions.

86. That was in the year 1535, and according to their plan the companions were to set out in 1537, on the feast of the Conversion of Saint Paul. But because war had broken out they set out in November 1536. Being about to depart, the pilgrim learned that an accusation had been brought before the inquisitor

This event bound the seven together into a fellowship based on a common ideal and mutual love, but as yet they had no thought of forming a religious congregation. What took place in the crypt that morning was only the seed of what would eventually blossom into the Society of Jesus.

Ignatius and his companions continued in their study of theology with the Dominicans, and then on March 14, 1535, Ignatius was granted his master's diploma, entitling him to be known henceforth as Master Ignatius.[34] During these past few months of study Ignatius' health had been growing progressively worse and the attacks he suffered were becoming more frequent. Though Ignatius did not want to interrupt his studies, nevertheless the physicians he consulted, as well as his companions, all agreed that since medical remedies proved ineffective, the only hope for him was to return to Azpeitia where his native air might accomplish what medicine had failed to do. This visit to Spain would also give Ignatius the opportunity to visit the families of the Spaniards in his group and inform the families of the manner of life their sons had chosen to follow. He could assure them that all was well and that they ought not put any trust in any rumors they may

and that a process was being initiated against him. Knowing this fact, although they were not summoning him, he himself went to the inquisitor and told him what he had heard, that he was about to depart for Spain, and that he had companions. So he asked him to pass sentence. The inquisitor said that with regard to an accusation being brought, that was true, but it did not appear to be anything important. He only wanted to see his writings, the Exercises. When he saw them he praised them highly and asked the pilgrim to leave a copy with him, and this he did. Nonetheless, he [the pilgrim] insisted that the process be carried out to the sentencing. Since the inquisitor offered excuses, he [the pilgrim] returned to his [the inquisitor's] residence with witnesses and a public notary who took down everyone's testimony.

have heard coming from Paris. Ignatius also wanted to see his friends Arteaga, Calixto, Castro, and Peralta, for he still harbored the hope that they might now join his group.

Since Ignatius was soon to leave them, the companions decided that they would leave Paris on January 25, 1537, to meet Ignatius in Venice and then the group could make its way to Jerusalem. Toward the end of March 1535 Ignatius was again denounced to the Inquisition because he continued to give the Exercises to those requesting them, and because his group regularly attended services at the Carthusian monastery and went to confession and received Holy Communion every week. Though he had not been summoned, Ignatius nevertheless went to visit the inquisitor, talked to him, and asked that his case be adjudicated as soon as possible since he was about to depart for Spain. The inquisitor, Valentín Liévin,[35] assured him that nothing serious had been brought against him, but having heard about his book, the Exercises, he very much wanted to see it. Ignatius handed him a copy and when the inquisitor had read through it and found nothing in it that merited censure he praised it, and as far as he was concerned the case was over. But Ignatius did not want to leave any suspicion hanging over his companions while he was away, and hence he asked that a favorable sentence be given. The inquisitor was reluctant to do so, thinking it not necessary, but Ignatius hired his own public notary, brought him and a few witnesses to the Dominican monastery where the inquisitor lived, and there the notary recorded the inquisitor's approval of Ignatius, of his group, and of the Exercises. Ignatius was now free to leave Paris and to return to Azpeitia; he had not seen his home for thirteen years.

Chapter 9

Spain: A Return Visit Home
(April–December 1535)

87. After he had completed this, he mounted the small horse his companions had purchased for him and set out alone for his homeland. On the way he found that he was feeling better. When he arrived in his province, he left the main road and took the mountain road because it was less traveled. After traversing a short distance he noticed two armed men coming toward him (that road is well known for its assassins), and after they had passed him by they turned around and came rushing after him so that he was somewhat afraid. Nevertheless, he spoke

---

87. In early April 1535, shortly after Easter (March 28), Ignatius left Paris to return to Spain; his constant companion on the trip was the small horse that his friends insisted he take because of his poor health. Since Ignatius followed the route that passed through Bayonne, which was one of the major stops on the way to Compostela, it is probable that he had followed that pilgrim route ever since leaving Paris.[1] He crossed into Spain at Irún and being within the borders of his home province of Guipúzcoa, he left the highway for the side roads that would take him through the mountains. This way he would not only enjoy the undulating landscapes of his beloved homeland, but he would be less likely to meet anyone who might recognize him. When he encountered the two armed servants, he was indeed glad to learn that they were not cutthroats, and was surprised that the news of his coming had already reached his brother, Martín García, at Loyola Castle. Unknown to Ignatius, he had been recognized in Bayonne,[2] and the news was speedily sent back to his family. Since Ignatius was returning to Azpeitia as a pilgrim and not as the courtier he once had been, he declined to live in the ancestral castle and chose to stay in the humble Hospital de la Magdalena, a hospice for the poor on the outskirts of Azpeitia, and in exchange for lodging he gave them his horse.[3]

to them and learned that they were his brother's servants and that his brother had despatched them to find him since his brother had received news of his coming, it seems, from Bayonne in France, where someone had recognized the pilgrim. As they went on ahead, he followed along the same road. He met the aforementioned men traveling toward him a little before arriving in his home territory. The men stubbornly insisted that they take him to his brother's house, but they were unable to convince him to go. He thus went to the hospital, and when it was convenient for him, he went out to seek alms in the region.

88. At this hospital he began to speak about the things of God to the many individuals who came to visit him, and through God's grace much fruit resulted. No sooner had he

88-89. In Azpeitia Ignatius returned to his earlier practice of daily catechism for the children, and since adults were also coming he arranged to speak to them three times a week. Because his explanation of the faith proved to be popular they soon became daily instructions, and since the number of people attending was ever growing, he moved his talks from the hospital into the open air. On Sundays and feast days he still preached in the church. There are two reasons for Ignatius' popularity. First, the faithful in Azpeitia were starving for the food of the soul; sermons were rarely heard in the parish church, even though there were some dozen priests associated with it.[4] Second, when Ignatius spoke about God and the things of God, he not only did so with sincerity and conviction, but it was evident to the people that he himself had experienced God, and that the flames that engulfed his heart were igniting theirs.

Though Ignatius spent only three months in Azpeitia he had accomplished much, not only in feeding the people with spiritual food, but also in seeing that certain pious customs were initiated and certain abuses eliminated. To assist the poor who were ashamed to beg, Ignatius persuaded the city magistrate and town council to draw up ordinances providing for the regular distribution of food for the poor.[5] An ordinance was also passed that church bells be rung at the time of the Angelus to remind the people to pray for those in mortal sin.[6] As for the abuses he helped eliminate, the first was gambling,[7] to which the people of Azpeitia were especially addicted, and which was the cause of some of the poverty in that area; he also helped terminate the custom of making shameful concubinage socially acceptable.[8]

arrived than he decided to teach Christian doctrine to the children daily, but his brother especially opposed this idea, saying no one would come. He replied that one would be enough. But after he had begun teaching many continually came to hear him, as did his brother.

Besides teaching Christian doctrine, he used to preach on Sundays and feast days with benefit and profit to the souls who came many miles to hear him. He also tried to eliminate some abuses and with God's help he corrected some of them. For example: he persuaded the magistrate of justice to ban gambling and to see that the law was observed. There was still another abuse, and it was this: the young girls of that region always go about with heads uncovered and only cover their heads when they marry. But there are many women who have become mistresses to priests and to other men, and are faithful to them as if they were their wives. This practice is so common that these mistresses have not the least shame in saying that they have covered their heads for so and so, and are accepted as so and so's wife.

89. Such a custom breeds many evils. The pilgrim persuaded the governor to pass a law that all who had covered their heads for someone, and were not their wives, should be punished according to the demands of justice. In this way the abuse began to be eliminated. He saw that an ordinance was passed so that

Sometime during his stay Ignatius' chronic stomach pain returned with its usual fever, but once it had passed he thought it time to move on and fulfill the requests that his companions had made of him to visit their families, and then make his way to Italy where he hoped to continue his study of theology while waiting for his companions to arrive. When Martín García learned that Ignatius was about to leave and intended to travel on foot and without money, he was embarrassed. To him it was unthinkable that Ignatius, a Loyola, should thus publicly shame his family. A Loyola had to travel on horse and with a retinue. Rather than cause his brother undue distress and in order to preserve peace, Ignatius finally yielded but only to this degree, that as long as he was traveling within the confines of Guipúzcoa, he would do so on horse and with an entourage.

the poor would be regularly provided for out of public funds, and that the bells be rung three times a day at the *Ave Maria*, that is, in the morning, at noon, and in the evening, so that the people can pray as they do in Rome.

Although he at first had been in good health, he later on became critically ill. Once his health returned, he decided to set out to fulfill the tasks that his companions had entrusted to him, and that he would go without any *quattrini*. His brother was greatly disturbed at this decision, and was embarrassed that he wanted to go on foot. By the time evening came the pilgrim had agreed to this: to travel to the provincial border on horseback, and together with his brother and relatives.

90. But when he passed the province boundary he dismounted, and taking nothing with him, headed for Pamplona;

90. Ignatius said good-by to his brother, whom he was never to see again, and continued his journey penniless and on foot. He was on his way to Obanos to deliver a letter to Juan de Azpilcueta, Xavier's brother, but before reaching Obanos he had to pass through Pamplona. Gazing at the city ramparts he remembered what had happened there fourteen years ago, and thanked God, who always works in mysterious ways, for calling him unto Himself. After delivering Xavier's letter, he walked southward to Almazán to Laínez' family, who greatly rejoiced when they heard that their son was to become a priest. In their joy they offered Ignatius money and a horse for his travels, but these he politely refused. He then went further south to Sigüenza to meet some unknown acquaintance of his, then toward Madrid. Since the royal family was in residence Ignatius paid a visit to Doña Leonor Mascarenhas, still acting as governess to the youthful Prince Philip who, fifty years later, remembered that he had once met the pilgrim.[9] In Madrid he surely visited Arteaga, who was tutor to the son of Don Juan de Zúñiga, Commander of Castile.[10] Ignatius still hoped to add his earlier companions to his group, but in this he had no success.

Ignatius then visited Toledo to see Salmerón's family,[11] as well as Master Peralta (see #78), now associated with the church in that city. He continued his journey in a southeasterly direction until he came to Valencia and learned that Master Castro (see #78) had recently entered the Carthusian Order; Ignatius went to visit him at the Charterhouse of Val de Cristo. He remained a guest of the monastery for eight days and then went to live with

and from there to Almazán, the hometown of Father Laínez; then to Sigüenza and Toledo; and from Toledo to Valencia. In all these hometowns of his companions he would not take anything, though a great deal had been offered to him and with great insistence.

In Valencia he spoke with Castro, who was a Carthusian monk. He wanted to board ship for Genoa, but his devoted friends in Valencia begged him not to, because they said that Barbarossa was at sea with his many galleys, etc. Though they had told him enough things to frighten him, still, nothing could make him change his mind.

91. He boarded a large vessel and lived through the storm previously mentioned, when he said that he had been three times at the point of death.

When he arrived in Genoa, he took the road to Bologna and on his way he suffered a great deal, especially on one occasion when he lost his way and began to walk alongside a river;

Martín Pérez de Almazán, Castro's friend.[12] It was now November and time for Ignatius to look to Italy. When his Valencian friends heard that he was planning on taking ship to Genoa, they tried their utmost to dissuade him, telling him that the waters off Spain were infested with the ships of that red-bearded pirate, Khair ed-Din,[13] more popularly known in Europe as Barbarossa. But no matter what they told him, or how urgently they insisted, Ignatius would not change his plans because of fear.

91. Ignatius boarded the ship for Genoa, but somewhere on the Mediterranean the ship met a storm of such severity that its rudder was broken (see #33) and everyone aboard felt certain that they were to die at sea. Through God's providence the damaged vessel landed in Genoa in mid-November, and Ignatius immediately started on his 180-mile journey to Bologna. Since Bologna boasted of a famous university, and the school year had just begun, Ignatius thought of spending the coming year there continuing his study of theology. On his way to Bologna he somehow lost his way, and on one occasion found himself traveling an extremely narrow path that hugged the edge of a cliff. Successfully extricating himself from that predicament, he continued until he was on the city's outskirts, and as he was crossing a foot bridge he fell into the cold muddy waters below. In clothes covered with mud, Ignatius made his entrance into that famous city,

the river was far below while the path was high above it. The farther he walked along the path, the narrower it became. It became so narrow that he could neither go ahead nor turn around and go back. He began to crawl on all fours and in this fashion he covered a good distance, but with much fear because every time he moved he thought he was going to fall into the river. This was the greatest physical strain and exertion he had ever experienced, but in the end he made it. As he was about to enter Bologna and was crossing over a small wooden bridge, he fell off of it. Thus, as he arose covered with mud and water he made the bystanders break out in laughter.

He entered Bologna and began to beg alms and got not even a single *quattrino*, though he had tried everywhere. He stayed in Bologna for some time because he was ill, then he went to Venice, always traveling in the same manner.

but his every attempt at begging proved unsuccessful. He did learn where the Spanish College was located—it was named San Clemente[14]—and there his countrymen gave him food and lodging. In mid-December he again suffered from acute pain in the stomach, so much so that he remained bedridden for a week. When he finally recovered he realized that it was the climate in Bologna that was causing him distress, so he relinquished the idea of studying at the university and judged it better to go to Venice. Thus, he set out after Christmas[15] and arrived in Venice at the end of 1535.

Chapter 10

Venice and Vicenza:
Awaiting Passage to the Holy Land
(January 1536–November 1537)

92. During his time in Venice he occupied himself giving the Exercises and in other spiritual conferences. The more illustrious persons to whom he gave them were Master Pietro Contarini and Master Gasparo de Dotti, and a Spaniard whose

92. In Venice Ignatius stayed with Andrea Lippomani,[1] prior of La Santissima Trinità, a poor but holy and learned man. Since Venice had no university — the Venetians attended that of Padua, some twenty-three miles away — Ignatius continued his study of theology privately, and in addition to the books that he had bought for himself he enjoyed the use of Lippomani's excellent library. Besides studying, he was also engaged in carrying on spiritual conversations with clergy and laypersons, and in giving the Exercises to those whom he judged ready. Among the several whom Ignatius had led through the Exercises, he mentions four. Master Pietro Contarini[2] was a noble Venetian cleric whose family had given several doges to the Venetian Republic, and Master Gasparo de Dotti[3] was vicar general to Girolamo Verallo, papal legate in Venice. The Spaniard Rozas[4] remains unidentified, and Bachelor Hoces,[5] another Spaniard, was friendly with Ignatius and with Gian Pietro Carafa, co-founder of the Theatines and former Bishop of Chieti.[6] That Hoces was at first reluctant to make the Exercises is perhaps attributable to Carafa, who heartily disliked Spaniards because, as a Neapolitan, he did not appreciate their having control of his native land, and it seems that he likewise bore a special animosity toward Ignatius himself.[7] Hoces finally made the Exercises and realized that all that had been told him about Ignatius and the Exercises was untrue, and thus he joined Ignatius' enterprise. He died in early 1538 while preaching in Padua, and Ignatius, involved in giving the Exercises at Monte Cassino (see #98), saw his soul enter heaven.

name was Rozas. There was also another Spaniard there named Bachelor Hoces who had many dealings with the pilgrim and also with the Bishop of Chieti. And though he had some inclination to make the Exercises, still, he didn't do anything about it. He finally decided to begin making them, and after three or four days into them, he opened his soul to the pilgrim, telling him that because of the things that someone had told him he was afraid that some villainous doctrine would be taught him in the Exercises. This was why he had brought certain books with him so that he could refer to them if, by chance, anyone wanted to deceive him. He was singularly helped by the Exercises and at their end he decided to follow the pilgrim's manner of life. He was also the first to die.

93. The pilgrim suffered another persecution while in Venice, with many saying that his effigy had been burned in Spain and

93. It appears that Ignatius was reluctant to reveal the name of the individual responsible for this persecution. Jerónimo Nadal, however, indicates in a letter of his that "opposition, spurred on by Pietro Carafa, arose in Venice"[8] against Ignatius. Whether Carafa was the cause of this persecution remains problematical, but certainly when Ignatius gave his reasons for not going to Rome with his companions in the spring of 1537, the new Theatine cardinal — Carafa became cardinal in December 1536 — was one of the reasons. The Venetian campaign against Ignatius ended with his being brought to trial, but the final sentence was in Ignatius' favor.[9]

While Ignatius was in Spain and in Venice, his six companions in Paris had increased their number to nine. In 1535, Claude Jay,[10] a Savoyard, made the Exercises under Faber and joined the group, and in 1536 Paschase Broët[11] and Jean Codure[12] did the same. The original plan was that the group was to depart Paris for Venice on January 25, 1537, but since hostilities between France and Spain were renewed in 1536, and since Charles V had attacked Marseilles and had his forces in Holland invade the north of France, the Parisians were filled with anti-Spanish sentiments. With half of the companions being Spaniards, they decided to anticipate the date of their departure. The route to Italy through southern France was out of the question, and so they chose to go through the neutral Duchy of Lorraine and Germany. A circuitous route, to be sure, but a safer route. Half of them left on November 11, 1536, and went as far as Meaux to await the others.

in Paris. This affair reached such a point that he was brought to trial and a sentence, favorable to the pilgrim, was given.

The nine companions arrived in Venice at the beginning of 1537. They split up so as to help out in different hospitals.

The remaining companions left the City of Light on November 15, met their friends at Meaux and started their two-month journey. They entered Germany at Zabern, then took the road to Basel, Constance, Trent, and finally the nine arrived in Venice on January 8, 1537, two months ahead of schedule.

Just as Faber had three recruits (Jay, Broët, and Codure), to introduce to Ignatius, the latter also had three recruits to present to his newly arrived friends. These new recruits of Ignatius were Diego de Hoces, and the Eguía brothers, Diego and Esteban. The latter two had recently returned from the Holy Land and unexpectedly found Ignatius, whom they had previously known in Alcalá (see #57); they made the Exercises under his supervision and then expressed their desire to join him after they had settled their affairs in Spain.[13] Since the group would have to wait for the pilgrim ship to take them to the Holy Land—and it was not due to come until sometime in June or July—the ten companions in Venice broke up into two groups and went to help in two of Venice's hospitals, that of Santi Giovanni e Paolo and that for the incurables. Ignatius, however, remained tied to his books since he was eager to finish his studies in time to be ordained before leaving for the Holy Land. The priests among them heard the confessions of the sick and prepared them for death, while the nonpriests busied themselves in sweeping floors, making beds, washing patients and bedpans, digging graves and burying the dead. For two months they worked in the hospitals and when March came it was time to seek papal approval for their pilgrimage to Jerusalem and to request ordination for the nonpriests among them.

The companions left Venice on March 16, desirous of being in the Eternal City for Holy Week and Easter. Ignatius remained behind with his books, thinking that his presence would only excite the ire of Cardinal Carafa, who was at the papal court, and Doctor Ortiz,[14] who was also in Rome. The companions arrived in Rome on Palm Sunday, March 25. They secured lodging at the Spanish hospice and met Doctor Ortiz who, when he had been informed of the purpose of their visit, not only showed interest in their cause but also manifested great benevolence toward them, for it was he who informed the pope that several masters from the Univer-

After two or three months they all went to Rome to obtain the blessing for their journey to Jerusalem. The pilgrim did not go because of Doctor Ortiz and also because of the new Theatine cardinal. The companions returned from Rome with drafts of 200 or 300 *escudos*, which had been given them as alms for their passage to Jerusalem. They were unwilling to take anything except drafts, and later, when they were not able to go to Jerusalem, they returned the drafts to those who had given them.

The companions returned to Venice in the same way that they had gone, that is, on foot and begging their way, but they were divided into three groups, in such a way that each group was made up of different nationalities. There in Venice, those who were not ordained were ordained for Mass, and the nuncio, who was then in Venice and who was later known as Cardinal Verallo, granted them faculties. They were ordained under the title of poverty and everyone took vows of poverty and chastity.

---

sity of Paris were in the city seeking audience. In response to Doctor Ortiz' request, the pope immediately set April 3, Easter Tuesday, as the date for their meeting. The encounter was most pleasant and the pope so genuinely enjoyed their conversation and discussion that when the audience was nearing its end he approved their pilgrimage and offered them sixty ducats to help pay their passage, and granted permission for the ordination of the nonpriests, but he then added that tension was growing in the Mediterranean so that they might never reach Jerusalem. Imitating the pope's generosity, the cardinals present likewise made offerings toward the pilgrimage, so that the net result of that meeting, together with gifts from others, was 260 ducats.[15] They left Rome at the beginning of May and when they arrived in Venice they went back to their volunteer work at the hospitals. On June 24 Ignatius, with five others (Xavier, Laínez, Rodrigues, Bobadilla, and Codure; Salmerón was still too young), was ordained to the priesthood by Vincenzo Nigusanti, Bishop of Arbe in Dalmatia, but a resident of Venice; the nuncio, Girolamo Verallo,[16] granted the group extensive faculties permitting them to hear confessions, dispense sacraments, preach, and teach Scripture anywhere in the Venetian Republic.

94. Ships were not sailing to the East that year because the Venetians had broken off relations with the Turks. Seeing that the possibility of sailing was becoming more remote, they dispersed throughout the Veneto region to wait out the year as they had agreed, and if there were no sailing after the year had passed, they would go to Rome.

It fell to the pilgrim to go with Faber and Laínez to Vicenza. There they found a certain building outside the city that had neither doors nor windows. They stayed in it and slept on the bit of straw that they had brought. Twice a day two of them went out to seek alms in that locality and they returned with so little that they could hardly sustain themselves. They usually ate some cooked bread — when they had bread — and the one who stayed at home took care of the cooking. In this way they spent forty days attending to nothing but their prayers.

95. After the forty days had passed, Master Jean Codure ar-

94. Since the Mediterranean and the Adriatic were swarming with Turkish galleys, and since Venice was preparing for war with the sultan, it became increasingly unlikely that a pilgrim ship would be going to the Holy Land that summer. So the would-be pilgrims changed their plans and decided to wait until the following summer. In the meantime they prepared to celebrate their first Masses. The eleven of them broke up into groups of two and three, and, choosing by lot, went to several northern Italian cities to spend forty days in prayer prior to their Masses. But before leaving Venice, Ignatius returned to Doctor Ortiz the ducats collected in Rome and asked him to keep them until an opportunity for sailing would again present itself.[17] The companions left Venice on July 25, and Ignatius, Faber, and Laínez went to Vicenza, forty-three miles west of Venice. The others went to Monselice, Treviso, Bassano, and Verona.

About a mile beyond the Santa Croce gate of Vicenza, Ignatius and his little group came upon the abandoned monastery of San Pietro in Vivarolo,[18] and there they took up residence. That they had to go out and beg twice a day shows how little they collected on each attempt. Usually Ignatius remained at the monastery and prepared the meals of cooked bread;[19] he was again suffering from stomach pain and his eyes had become weak because of the many tears he shed in prayer.[20]

95. The forty days in Vicenza were days of incessant prayer and of in-

rived and the four of them decided to begin preaching. All four went to different squares in the city, and at the same hour of the same day they began their sermons by shouting loudly to the people and waving their birettas to call them together. These sermons caused much talk in the city and many persons were moved with devotion and abundantly supplied them with all that they materially needed.

During the period that he was in Vicenza, he received many spiritual visions and many rather ordinary consolations (it was just the opposite when he was in Paris), but especially when he began to prepare for his ordination in Venice and when he was getting ready to celebrate Mass. Also during his journeys

timate union with God, and during that period Ignatius was the recipient of many extraordinary graces, similar to those that he had while in Manresa. Such graces had been granted him in Venice when he was preparing for his ordination, and now in Vicenza as he was preparing to celebrate his first Mass. Toward the end of August, having received word from Bassano that Rodrigues was on his death bed, Ignatius and Faber went to visit him, and when they arrived their visit so consoled the sick man that he soon felt better.

The forty days were up on September 6, and shortly thereafter Codure joined them, coming from Treviso,[21] and all four went into the city to begin their apostolate of preaching. None of the four was fluent enough in Italian to be able to hold public discourse, but that did not deter them. Ignatius had been in Italy for eighteen months and when he began his discourse it was a mixture of French and Latin,[22] nevertheless, he and his companions made themselves understood so that the people not only became interested but returned to hear them, and responded generously by giving them alms.

All ten companions eventually convened at the deserted monastery outside Vicenza to evaluate their present situation. Since there would be no pilgrim ship going to the Holy Land that year, they all determined to wait for another year. What to do in the meantime? They were all university graduates and so they decided to go to the various university centers in Italy (Padua, Ferrara, Bologna, and Siena) and begin their apostolate of preaching and teaching, hearing confessions and giving the Exercises, etc.; perhaps they might win some new recruits from among the students. But he enjoyed great supernatural visitations of the kind that he used to have when he was in Manresa. While he was in Vicenza he learned that one of the companions, who was in Bassano, was at the point of death. Though he himself was ill with fever at that time, nevertheless, he started on the trip and walked so energetically that Faber, his companion, could not keep up with him. During that trip God gave him the assurance, and this he told to Faber, that the companion would not die from that illness. After he arrived at Bassano, the sick man was greatly consoled and quickly recovered.

Everyone then returned to Vicenza and all ten were there for some time and some went out begging alms in the towns around Vicenza.

96. They decided that after a year had passed, and if they still found no passage, they would go to Rome, and the pilgrim too, because the last time the companions had gone there the

Ignatius, Faber, and Laínez were to go to Rome and do the same there.

Before dispersing, one final question had to be settled: if anyone should ask them to which congregation they belonged, or what they called themselves, what answer should they give? Ignatius suggested that they pray over it, and when the discussion was renewed everyone acknowledged that since no one among them was their head, but only Jesus Christ, and since it was Jesus whom they desired to serve, they ought to carry His name. Thus they decided on calling themselves *Compañía de Jesús*, but when that was rendered into Latin it became *Societas Jesu*, and when this is translated into English it becomes the familiar *Society of Jesus*.

96-97. The others who had been ordained with Ignatius in June had celebrated their first Masses in Vicenza sometime in September, but Ignatius chose to postpone his for another year. He still carried the hope that he might celebrate it in the Holy Land.

While waiting for the year to pass and hoping that the summer of 1538 would bring a pilgrim ship to Venice, the companions dispersed to the various cities while Ignatius went to Rome. He was no longer worried about Doctor Ortiz and Cardinal Carafa; the former had proven to be a friend when the companions were in Rome the previous year, and as for the latter, Ignatius had been vindicated in the trial that had been brought against him in Venice.

two men, about whom he had his doubts, had shown themselves most benevolent.

They went to Rome in three or four groups; the pilgrim was with Faber and Laínez, and on this journey God often visited him in a special way.

After he had been ordained a priest, he decided to wait another year before celebrating Mass, preparing himself and praying to our Lady to place him with her Son. One day, a few miles before reaching Rome, while praying in a church, he felt a great change in his soul and so clearly did he see God the Father place him with Christ, His Son, that he had no doubts that God the Father did place him with His Son.

97. Then on arriving in Rome he told the companions that he saw that the windows were closed, meaning by this that

According to their revised plan, the companions were to spend the winter preaching in the cities assigned to them and when spring came they were to come to Rome for further deliberation. Ignatius, Faber, and Laínez left Vicenza in October. This journey to Rome was Ignatius' final cross-country journey, and the three pilgrims, coming from Siena, approached Rome by the Via Cassia; about eight miles outside the city they came to the small village of La Storta. Since they were tired, but at the same time eager to get to Rome that evening, they chose to stop at the chapel, get some rest, do some praying, and then continue their way. When Ignatius relates the mystical experience that was his at La Storta, he merely gives the basic fact and omits all detail and embellishment. But from those who were with him we learn that as soon as Ignatius entered the chapel he felt a sudden change come over him, and while he was praying he had a remarkable vision. He saw God the Father together with Jesus, who was carrying His cross. Both Father and Son were looking most kindly upon him and he heard the Father say to the Son: "I wish you to take him as your servant." Jesus then directed His words to the kneeling pilgrim and said: "I wish you to be our servant." This was exactly what Ignatius had always wanted. Then he heard the Father add: "I will be favorable to you in Rome."[23] This was God's answer to Ignatius' frequent prayer that he be placed next to Mary's Son. Leaving the chapel and continuing his way to Rome, Ignatius did not know whether he would meet success or persecution, but he knew that God would be with him.

they would have to suffer many contradictions. He likewise said: "We must always be on our guard, and hold no conversations with women, unless they be ladies of prominence." Later in Rome, to continue on this same subject, Master Francis heard a woman's confession and once visited her to speak to her of spiritual matters. She was later found to be pregnant, but it pleased the Lord that the man who had done the wicked deed was discovered. The same happened to Jean Codure, whose spiritual daughter was caught with a man.

Upon entering Rome he noticed that the windows in the buildings were closed and he interpreted this to mean that they would meet opposition and persecution, but having the assurance of divine protection, he knew those forces could not prevail over the Society of Jesus. Still, they were to be cautious, and Ignatius told them to be prudent when dealing with women. He then cited two examples of what happened to Xavier and Codure shortly after their arrival in Rome. To avoid such embarrassment in the future, Ignatius decided that no one was to hear the confessions of women in their homes without a companion.[24] .

Chapter 11

Rome: First Year in the Eternal City (1538)

98. From Rome the pilgrim went to Monte Cassino to give the Exercises to Doctor Ortiz. He was there for forty days and once during that period he saw Bachelor Hoces enter heaven, and as a result of this he shed many tears and had great spiritual consolation. He saw this so clearly that if he were to say the

98. In Rome, Ignatius and his companions were offered the use of an empty house in the vineyard on the estate of Quirino Garzoni, and there they made their home.[1] The building was located on Monte Pincio, near the church Trinità dei Monti, where Faber and Laínez celebrated daily Mass. Pope Paul III remembered that they were university-trained theologians, and thus he appointed Faber and Laínez to teach Scripture and theology at Rome's Sapienza College, while he left Ignatius free to carry on his particular apostolate of preaching and giving the Exercises. Among the first to make the Exercises was Doctor Ortiz, who was now one of Ignatius' most enthusiastic supporters.

At the beginning of March 1538, Ignatius and Doctor Ortiz traveled the eighty-eight miles to Monte Cassino and in the nearby dependent priory of Santa Maria dell' Albaneta[2] Ignatius and the Doctor prayed for forty days. On their return trip to Rome they met a young Spaniard whom Ignatius knew, Francisco Estrada,[3] who was on his way to Naples to join the military. Ignatius persuaded him to return to Rome, where he made the Exercises and eventually entered the Society. Among the others whom Ignatius led through the Exercises, the more prominent were Cardinal Gasparo Contarini,[4] who always remained a faithful friend of the Society, and the humanist ambassador from Siena, Lattanzio Tolomei. There were others as well, scattered throughout Rome, and by mentioning that one retreatant lived near Santa Maria Maggiore and another by Ponte Sisto, Ignatius is telling us that each day he had to go from one end of the city to the other in order to lead his retreatants through their meditations.

contrary he would feel as though he were lying. From Monte Cassino he brought back with him Francisco Estrada.

When he returned to Rome he kept himself busy helping souls, and while still living at the vineyard he gave the Spiritual Exercises to several individuals at one and the same time. One

Ignatius had asked all the companions to be in Rome for Easter, since it was almost certain that there would be war and that any chance of going to the Holy Land was becoming more and more remote. After they had arrived the companions went to various churches in Rome and began their preaching; Ignatius went to that of Santa Maria di Monserrato, since that was the Spanish church and there he would be able to preach in Spanish. The principal content of these sermons were the fundamentals of the Catholic faith, but with a view to correcting the Lutheran teaching that an Augustinian friar, Agostino Mainardi,[5] had expounded in his sermons during Lent. Since the companions were trying to undo the harm that Mainardi had done, some of the latter's followers — three Spaniards in the Roman Curia, Francisco de Mudarra, a certain Barreda, and Pedro de Castilla[6] — concocted vicious lies about Ignatius and his companions and planted them throughout the city. Thus began a persecution which Ignatius judged to be the most severe that he had ever undergone.[7] The story was passed on that Ignatius and his companions were disguised Lutherans who by the Exercises intended to teach erroneous doctrine, and that they had come to Rome after they had been forced to flee Spain, Paris, and Venice, where they were wanted by the authorities for their false teaching and immoral living. Though Mudarra and friends never brought a formal charge against Ignatius, nevertheless, the slander they sowed had its effect for the people now avoided them and were afraid to attend their sermons. Mudarra brought Miguel Landívar[8] into the picture by telling the governor, Benedetto Conversini,[9] that Miguel had known Ignatius in Paris, and that he would reveal all secrets.

Ignatius appeared before Conversini carrying a letter that the same Miguel had written to him in Vicenza, dated September 12, 1537.[10] When the governor perused Miguel's letter, in which he not only praised Ignatius but requested to join his group, Conversini immediately approached Miguel on the matter. Face to face with his own written testimony, Miguel admitted tht he had been telling lies and the governor consequently banished him from Rome.

Since Ignatius had won the first skirmish, Mudarra was not willing to leave the field of battle and thus he continued to spread his slanderous lies.

of these lived near Santa Maria Maggiore, and another near Ponte Sisto.

Then the persecutions began. Miguel started trouble by speaking ill of the pilgrim and had him summoned before the governor. The pilgrim first showed the governor one of Miguel's

As long as Ignatius was without a clear acquittal, the Romans continued to stay away from him and his companions. Since their apostolate had been severely diminished, Ignatius returned to Conversini and requested that his accusers be brought forward to prove their accusations publicly and this the governor agreed to do. When Mudarra and friends were before the governor and papal legate, Cardinal Gian Vincenzo Carafa,[11] they realized that they had now lost the battle and willingly acknowledged that they knew of nothing in Ignatius' teaching or way of life that was heretical or scandalous. With this admission the governor and legate suggested that the case be dropped, but Ignatius insisted that a final sentence be rendered, for without such a sentence the spectre of heresy would always overshadow them and their labors. In order for their helping souls to bear fruit, an official exoneration was imperative, but Conversini did not see eye to eye with Ignatius and so nothing was done about it.

Ignatius bided his time until Paul III returned to Rome in mid-August. The pope had been to Nice mediating a truce between Charles V and Francis I, and in the latter part of that month he went to his summer residence in Frascati. The determined Ignatius went to Frascati, secured an audience and explained everything to His Holiness. Ignatius narrated the plans that he and his companions had in mind, and related how he had been the victim of the Inquisition in Alcalá and Salamanca. He held nothing back. Finally, he asked that a complete investigation be made into their doctrine and lifestyle, and that a sentence eventually be published. Under papal command, Conversini again took up the process and after weeks of thorough investigation nothing was found heretical in Ignatius' teaching or in his manner of life and, finally, the long-awaited sentence was published on November 18, 1538.[12]

With a favorable sentence to their credit, the companions, following the vow they had made in Montmartre (that if unable to go to the Holy Land they would place themselves at the pope's disposal), went to visit Paul III sometime after the 18th and before the 23rd of November. They offered themselves and their services to the pope for the good of the Church, saying that they were willing to go wherever the pope should decide to send them and do whatever work the pope should decide to entrust to them.

letters in which he enthusiastically praised him; the governor then interrogated Miguel and the outcome was that he was banished from Rome.

Then Mudarra and Barreda began their persecution, alleging that the pilgrim and his companions were fugitives from

The pontiff accepted their humble offering and within months he was to call on Ignatius and these same companions to supply missionaries to go to Siena, Parma, and even India.

Since Ignatius' desire to celebrate his first Mass in the very land where Jesus had lived had never come to pass, he did the next best thing. At Santa Maria Maggiore in Rome, there was a Chapel of the Manger where a relic of Bethlehem was preserved, and there Ignatius and his companions went on Christmas eve 1538. Surrounded by his closest friends and with eyes so filled with tears that he could hardly read the missal, Ignatius celebrated the Mass he so long desired to celebrate.

After Ignatius had narrated these events of 1538, he mentioned three particular works in which he had been instrumental in establishing in Rome. The first was an orphan society founded to distribute alms to the truly indigent — that is, to the sick, to beggars who were unable to work, and to orphans — and at the same time curb the growing number of professionally lazy beggars who wandered the Roman streets. The society was approved by Pope Paul III on February 7, 1541. The second work of mercy that the early Jesuits sponsored was a residence for fallen girls and wives who were in moral danger, where they were rehabilitated and prepared for positions in the world and for proper marriages. The papal bull establishing such a residence was issued on February 16, 1543, and when the residence opened the following January Ignatius named it after Saint Martha. Though the everyday operation of the residence was in the hands of a confraternity founded especially for this purpose, Ignatius had charge of the spiritual government of the house. The final work of piety that Ignatius mentions was the establishment of a house for catechumens. Many Jews and Muslims in Rome, who desired to become Catholics, found that as long as they nurtured this desire they were unable to remain at home; hence they lived together in a residence where the Jesuits served as catechists. This apostolate received the pope's approbation on February 19, 1543.

Realizing that Gonçalves da Câmara would shortly be leaving Rome for Spain and being unable to complete his narration, Ignatius told him that Master Nadal would fill him in on all that remained, for Nadal was also going to Spain and was to be Gonçalves da Câmara's companion.

Spain, from Paris, and from Venice. In the end, both of them confessed in the governor's presence and that of the legate, who was then in Rome, that they had nothing bad to say about them, nor about their life-style, nor about their teaching. The legate ordered silence to be imposed on the entire affair, but the pilgrim did not agree to this, but said that he wanted a definitive sentence issued. This was not to the legate's liking, nor to that of the governor, nor to those who were, from the beginning, well-disposed toward the pilgrim. Finally, after several months, the pope returned to Rome. The pilgrim went to speak with him at Frascati and set forth his several reasons, and the pope, now fully informed, ordered that sentence be given, and it was favorable to him, and so forth.

Through the pilgrim's help and that of his companions several works of piety were initiated in Rome, for example, the house for catechumens, that of Saint Martha, the orphan society, etc. As for the rest, Master Nadal can tell you about that.

99. After he had narrated these matters, I asked the pilgrim on October 20, about the Exercises and the Constitutions because I wanted to know how he had written them. He told me that he had not composed the Exercises all at one time,

99-101. Now that Ignatius had finished his story, Gonçalves da Câmara hurriedly asked him about the composition of the Spiritual Exercises and the Constitutions. As for the former, Ignatius said that they were written over a period of time, and were based on his own experiences in prayer. Whatever he found helpful he recorded so that these same exercises might prove helpful to others. The Constitutions were likewise written under the influence of prayer, for when Ignatius celebrated Mass he would present the point under consideration to God and request enlightenment, and if he were coming to a decision, he asked for confirmation. During the years he was occupied in writing the Constitutions and perfecting them, Ignatius was the recipient of countless mystical graces from God, all of which he recorded in his *Spiritual Journal,*[13] of which only a fragment remains today, covering the time between February 2, 1544, and February 27, 1545. This fragment appears to be much less than that "large packet of writings" from which Ignatius read excerpts to Goncalves da Câmara. It is unknown but perceiving certain things happening in his soul, and finding them helpful, he thought that they might also be helpful to others and so he set them down in writing, for example, the examination of conscience with its series of lines, etc. He told me that he had especially derived the elections from that diversity of spirits and thoughts he experienced when he was at Loyola, still suffering with his bad leg. As for the Constitutions, he told me that he would speak to me about them that evening.

That same day, before supper, he called for me and seemed to be more recollected than usual. He made a solemn avowal, the gist of which was to inform me that his intention had been to be sincere in all that he had related; that he was certain that he did not exaggerate in anything; that he had often offended God after he had begun to serve Him but had never consented to mortal sin; and that his devotion, that is, his ease in finding God, was always increasing, now more than ever in his entire life. At whatever time or hour he wanted to find God, he found Him. Also that he now has many visions, especially those, as have been mentioned above, of seeing Christ as the sun. This often occurred when he was speaking of important matters and those visions came to him as corroborations.

100. When he celebrated Mass he also had many visions, and when he was writing the Constitutions he had them quite frequently. This he can prove very easily because every day he noted what was taking place in his soul and all this is found written down. He then showed me a rather large packet of writings and from these he read to me a sizeable amount. For the most part they were visions that he had had confirming certain points in the Constitutions. Sometimes he saw God the

how the greater part of the journal became lost, or whether Ignatius himself had destroyed it. Certainly, when Gonçalves da Câmara asked to take these writings to his room to read at his leisure, Ignatius would not part with them. He probably felt that he had already revealed more than he had intended to reveal.

Father, at other times all three Persons of the Trinity, and at other times our Lady, who was at times interceding for him and at times strengthening him.

He especially spoke to me about certain items under deliberation and for which he celebrated Mass every day for forty days and had daily shed many tears. The question was whether a church should have any income, and if the Society could make use of that income.

101. The method he followed when writing the Constitutions was to celebrate Mass every day and present the point under consideration to God and to pray over it. He always had tears when he prayed or celebrated Mass.

I wanted to see all those papers on the Constitutions and asked him to let me have them for a while, but he would not.

Appendix I
Preface of Father Nadal[1]

1. I, and many other fathers, have heard our Father Ignatius say that he had asked God to grant him three graces before departing this life. First, that the Apostolic See confirm the Institute of the Society; second, the same for the Spiritual Exercises; third, that he be able to write the Constitutions.

2. Remembering this, and seeing that he had received all three graces,[2] I began to fear that he would be called from us to go to a better life. Since I knew that the holy father-founders of monastic communities had been accustomed to leave their sons some admonition, as a testament, to help them grow in virtue, I waited for the opportune moment to ask the same of Father Ignatius.

One day in 1551,[3] when we were together, Father Ignatius said to me: "Just now I was higher than heaven." I understood this to mean that he had experienced some ecstasy or rapture, as it frequently happened to him. With the deepest respect I asked him: "Father, what do you mean?" But he changed the conversation to something else. Thinking that this was the suitable moment, I begged the Father to be kind enough to tell us how the Lord had guided him from the beginning of his conversion, so that his explanation could serve us as a testament and paternal instruction. Thus, I said to him: "Since God has granted you the three graces you desired before your death, we fear, Father, that you will soon be called to heaven."

3. The Father offered business matters as his excuse, saying that he had neither the inclination nor the time for it. He added, however: "Offer three Masses for this intention, you, Polanco,[4] and Ponce,[5] and after you have prayed tell me what you think." I answered: "Father, we will be of the same opinion as we now are." But he replied with great gentleness: "Do what I tell you!" We celebrated the three Masses and reported to him that we were of the same mind, and he then promised to do what we had asked.

The following year,[6] after I had again returned from Sicily, and being about to be sent to Spain, I asked the Father if he had done anything. "Nothing," he said. When I returned from Spain in 1554, I asked him once more. He had not yet begun.[7] I do not know what impelled me, but I insisted with the Father: "It is now going on four years that not only have I asked you, but also other fathers, for you to explain to us, Father, how

123

the Lord had formed you from the beginning of your conversion, for we are confident that knowing this would be most beneficial to us and to the Society. But since I see that you will not grant it to us, I dare to make this statement: If you grant the request we so earnestly desire, we will put it to our best use, and if you do not grant it, our spirits will not be thereby dejected, but we will have the same confidence in the Lord as if you had written everything down."

4. The Father did not answer anything, but — I think it was the same day — he called Father Luis Gonçalves to him and began his narration. This father, endowed with an excellent memory, afterward wrote it down. This Father Luis was an elector at the General Congregation,[8] and at the same he was elected assistant to Father General Laínez. Later he became tutor in literature and Christian morals to Sebastian, King of Portugal. He is a father known for his piety and outstanding virtue. Father Gonçalves wrote a part in Spanish and a part in Italian, depending on the scribes he had at his disposal. Father Annibal du Coudret,[9] a learned and pious man, made the Latin translation. Both the author and the translator are still alive.

Appendix II

Chronology of Events in the Life of Ignatius Loyola

1491		– born at Loyola Castle, sometime prior to October 23
1506(?)		– in service as page to Juan Velázquez de Cuéllar of Arévalo, treasurer to King Ferdinand
1515		
Feb.	20	– youthful escapade in Azpeitia with charges subsequently brought against him
1517		
Aug.	12	– Juan Velázquez de Cuéllar dies
End of year		– in service to Antonio Manrique de Lara, Duke of Nájera, Viceroy of Navarre
1521		
Jan.-Apr.		– helps to bring peace to provincial factions in Guipúzcoa
May	17-18	– hastens to Pamplona to defend the city
	19	– convinces commander to defend fortress
	20	– right leg is wounded during siege
	23-24	– fortress at Pamplona surrenders to French

June	2-5	– leaves Pamplona for Loyola Castle
	17-20	– arrives at Loyola Castle
	24	– receives last sacraments
	28 midnight	– health begins to improve
Aug.-Sept.		– begins reading a life of Christ and those of the saints; undergoes conversion and has vision of our Lady

1522

End Feb.		– leaves Loyola on way to Montserrat
Mar.	21	– arrives at Montserrat
	22-24	– prepares for general confession
	24	– sets aside his fine clothing for pilgrim's tunic; at midnight begins vigil before our Lady's altar
	25	– early morning leaves Montserrat and arrives in Manresa where he lives life of prayer and penance
Aug.-Sept.(?)		– extraordinary illumination on the shores of the Cardoner and undergoes interior transformation; begins writing Spiritual Exercises

1523

Mid-Feb.		– departs Manresa
	17-18	– arrives in Barcelona on way to Holy Land
Mid-Mar.		– departs for Italy
	20-22	– arrives in Gaeta, Italy
	29	– arrives in Rome on Palm Sunday
Apr.	13-14	– departs for Venice
May	14(?)	– arrives in Venice
July	24	– departs for Cyprus
Aug.	19	– arrives at Las Salinas, Cyprus
	31	– arrives at Jaffa

Sept.	4	– arrives in Jerusalem
	23	– departs Jerusalem for Jaffa
Oct.	3	– departs Jaffa
	14	– arrives in Las Salinas, Cyprus
Early Nov.		– departs for Venice

1524

Mid-Jan.	– arrives in Venice
Early Feb.	– departs for Genoa and Barcelona
Late Feb.-	
early Mar.	– arrives in Barcelona, visits Manresa; begins studies; spends two years in Barcelona

1526

| July(?) | | – goes to Alcalá to begin studies |
| Nov. | 19 | – first process initiated against Ignatius |

1527

Mar.	6	– second process in Alcalá
Apr.	18/19	– put into prison
May	2-21	– third process
June	1	– released from prison
	21	– departs Alcalá for Valladolid
Early July		– visits Archbishop Fonseca in Valladolid, then goes to Salamanca
Mid-July		– arrives in Salamanca
End July		– meets with Dominican friars at San Esteban, then imprisonment
Aug.	20-22	– released from prison
Mid-Sept.		– leaves Salamanca for Barcelona and then to Paris

1528

| Feb. | 2 | – arrives in Paris; begins Latin studies at Collège de Montaigu |

1529

Lent		– first begging tour in Flanders
Sept.		– visits Rouen
Oct.	1	– moves to Collège de Sainte-Barbe; meets Faber and Xavier and begins study of philosophy

1530

Aug.-Sept.   – second begging tour in Flanders

1531

Aug.-Sept.   – third begging tour in Flanders; visits London

1532

Jan.   – receives Bachelor of Arts degree

1533

Mar.   13   – examination for licentiate degree

1534

Jan.   – gives Exercises to Faber
Spring   – gives Exercises to Laínez and Salmerón; later to Rodrigues and Bobadilla
Aug.   15   – vows at Montmartre
Sept.   – gives Exercises to Xavier

1535

Mar.   14   – receives diploma of Master of Arts
Late Mar.   – defends himself against the accusation of heresy before Valentín Liévin
Early Apr.   – leaves Paris for Spain
End Apr.   – arrives in Azpeitia

Aug.-Sept.	– visits Obanos, Almazán, Sigüen- za, Madrid, Toledo, Valencia
Oct.-Nov.	– visits Charterhouse of Val de Cristo; leaves Valencia for Genoa
Mid-Nov.	– arrives Genoa, walks to Bologna
Dec. 11-18(?)	– ill in Bologna
End Dec.	– leaves Bologna; arrives Venice

1537

Jan. 8	– companions arrive from Paris and work in hospitals
Mar. 18	– companions leave for Rome while Ignatius remains in Venice
25	– arrival in Rome
Apr. 3	– audience with Pope Paul III
Early May	– leave Rome for Venice
Mid-May	– arrival in Venice
June 24	– Ignatius and five companions are ordained to priesthood
July 25	– Ignatius, Faber, and Laínez leave for Vicenza; others leave for other cities
End Aug.	– travels with Faber to Bassano to visit Rodrigues who is ill
Sept.-Oct.	– companions celebrate their first Masses in Vicenza; decide on their ministries and on the group's name
Oct. 13	– declaration of Ignatius' innocence given in Venice
End Oct.	– leaves with Faber and Laínez for Rome
Mid-Nov.	– vision at La Storta; arrives in Rome and lives near Trinità dei Monti

1538

| Mar.-Apr. | – at Monte Cassino giving Exer- cises to Pedro Ortiz |

End Apr.   – companions arrive in Rome;
                                        group moves to residence near
                                        Ponte Sisto
May   – persecution begins
End Aug.   – goes to Frascati to visit Pope
                                        Paul III and requests a definitive
                                        sentence
Nov.   18   – sentence exonerating Ignatius and
                                        companions published
Nov.   18–23   – the young Society offers its ser-
                                        vices to Pope Paul III in accord
                                        with the vow at Montmartre
Dec.   25   – Ignatius celebrates his first Mass
                                        in the Chapel of the Manger in
                                        Santa Maria Maggiore

1539

Mid March-
  June   24   – deliberations on whether to form
                                        a new religious congregation
End June-
  July   – Ignatius prepares Formula of the
                                        Institute
Sept.   3   – Pope Paul III grants oral
                                        approval to Formula of the
                                        Institute

1540

Sept.   27   – confirmation of the Society by
                                        papal bull *Regimini militantis
                                        Ecclesiae*

1541

Mar.   4   – first companions discuss the
                                        writing of Constitutions for the
                                        new Society
          10   – Ignatius and Codure given task
                                        of writing Constitutions

Apr.	8	– Ignatius is elected general, but declines
	13	– is again elected, but requests to spend some days in prayer
	19	– accepts election as general
	22	– Ignatius and companions make their solemn profession in Chapel of Our Lady in St. Paul Outside-the-Walls.

1543

Feb.	16	– papal bull establishing House of Saint Martha
	19	– papal bull establishing house for catechumens in Rome

1544

Jan.		– House of Saint Martha opens
Mar.	14	– papal bull, *Iniunctum nobis*, again confirms the Society and no longer limits its membership to 60

1545

June	3	– papal brief grants faculties and privileges to the Society

1546

June	5	– papal brief permits the Society to accept spiritual and temporal coadjutors
Oct.	1	– apostolic constitution forbids female branch of the Society
	25	– Portugal is made first province in the Society; Simón Rodrigues is named provincial

1547

May	7	– Ignatius writes letter on perfection
Sept.	1	– Antonio Araoz is named first provincial of Spain

1548

July	31	– Pope Paul III praises and approves the Spiritual Exercises

1549

Feb.	1	– first missionaries go to Brazil
	16	– preparations are made for Peter Canisius, Claude Jay, and Alfonso Salmerón to go to Germany
June	27	– Ignatius contemplates founding the Roman College and building a new church for the Society
Oct.	10	– India becomes a province with Francis Xavier as provincial

1550

July	21	– Pope Julius III's bull, *Exposcit debitum*, confirms the Society

1551

Jan.		– professed fathers gather in Rome to discuss Constitutions
	30	– because of ill health Ignatius submits his resignation, but not accepted
Feb.	22	– Roman College inaugurated
Aug.	1	– Ignatius contemplates establishing a German College in Rome
Dec.	5	– Italy becomes a province with Paschase Broët as provincial

1552

Jan.	1	– Aragón becomes a province with Simón Rodrigues provincial
Feb.	1	– Jerónimo Doménech made first provincial of Sicily
Mar.		– Ignatius finishes writing Constitutions
	25	– Jerónimo Nadal appointed to promulgate Constitutions in Sicily
Aug.	31	– papal bull establishes German College in Rome

1553

Mar.	26	– the famous letter on obedience to the Jesuits in Coimbra
Apr.	10	– Nadal appointed to promulgate Constitutions in Spain and Portugal
July	9	– Ignatius establishes Brazil as a province and names Emmanuel de Nóbrega provincial

1554

Jan.	7	– Spain divided into three provinces: Aragón, Castile, and Bética.
Jun.	14	– entrusts the construction of the Society's new church to Michelangelo Buonarotti
Oct.	6	– work begins on the church but continues only until 1555
Nov.	1	– Ignatius asks priests in Rome to chose a vicar general to assist him in governing the Society; he confirms the election of Jerónimo Nadal

1555

Aug.   – France is made a province

1556

June   7   – Peter Canisius appointed first
                                provincial of Germany
July   31   – Ignatius dies at 5:30 a.m.
Aug.   1   – buried in church of Our Lady
                                della Strada

1609

July   27   – beatified by Pope Paul V

1622

Mar.   12   – canonized by Pope Gregory XV

Appendix III
Select Bibliography

On Ignatius Loyola

Brodrick, James, S.J. *Saint Ignatius Loyola: The Pilgrim Years 1491-1538* (New York: Farrar, Straus and Cudahy, 1956).

Dudon, Paul, S.J. *St. Ignatius of Loyola*. Tr. William J. Young, S.J. (Milwaukee: Bruce, 1949).

Purcell, Mary. *The First Jesuit: St. Ignatius Loyola (1491-1556)* (Chicago: Loyola University, 1981).

Rahner, Hugo, S.J., and Leonard von Matt. *St. Ignatius of Loyola: A Pictorial Biography*. Tr. John Murray, S.J. (Chicago: Regnery, 1956).

Rahner, Karl, S.J., and Paul Imhof, S.J. *Ignatius of Loyola* (New York: Collins, 1979).

On Ignatian Spirituality

Brou, Alexandre. *The Ignatian Way to God*. Tr. William J. Young, S.J. (Milwaukee: Bruce, 1952).

Finding God in All Things: Essays in Ignatian Spirituality. Tr. William J. Young, S.J. (Chicago: Regnery, 1958).

Gill, Henry Vincent. *Jesuit Spirituality: Leading Ideas of the Spiritual Exercises* (Dublin: M. H. Gill, 1935).

Guibert, Joseph de. *The Jesuits: Their Spiritual Doctrine and Practice; a Historical Study*. Tr. William J. Young, S.J. Ed. George E. Ganss, S.J. (Chicago: Institute of Jesuit Sources, 1964).

Maruca, Dominic, S.J. *Instruments in the Hand of God: A Study in the Spirituality of St. Ignatius Loyola* (Rome: Gregorian University, 1963).

Peeters, Louis. *An Ignatian Approach to Divine Union*. Tr. Hillard L. Brozowski. (Milwaukee: Bruce, 1956).

Puhl, L. *The Spiritual Exercises of St. Ignatius: A New Translation* (Westminster, Md.: Newman, 1951).

Rahner, Hugo, S.J. *Ignatius the Theologian.* Tr. Michael Barry. (New York: Herder and Herder, 1968).

_____. *The Spirituality of St. Ignatius Loyola: An Account of Its Historical Development.* Tr. Francis John Smith, S.J. (Westminster, Md.: Newman, 1953).

Notes

Abbreviations used in Notes

FD   =   *Fontes Documentales de S. Ignatio de Loyola: Documenta de S. Ignatii familia et patria, iuventute, primis sociis (MHSI 115),* ed. Candidus de Dalmases, S.I. (Rome: Institutum Historicum Societatis Iesu, 1977).

FN   =   *Fontes Narrativi de S. Ignatio de Loyola et de Societatis Iesu initiis* 1: *Narrationes scriptae ante annum 1557 (MHSI 66),* ed. Dionysius Fernandez Zapico, S.I., and Candidus de Dalmases, S.I. (Rome: Monumenta Historica Soc. Iesu, 1943); 2: *Narrationes scriptae annis 1557-1574 (MHSI 73),* ed. Candidus de Dalmases, S.I. (Rome: Monumenta Historica Soc. Iesu, 1951).

FX   =   Schurhammer, Georg, S.J. *Francis Xavier, His Life, His Times* 1: *Europe 1506-1541.* Tr. M. Joseph Costelloe, S.J. (Rome: Jesuit Historical Institute, 1973).

IdL   =   Leturia, Pedro, S.J. *Iñigo de Loyola.* Tr. Aloysius J. Owen, S.J. (Syracuse: Le Moyne College, 1949).

IL   =   Dudon, Paul, S.J. *St. Ignatius of Loyola.* Tr. William J. Young, S.J. (Milwaukee: Bruce, 1949).

LIL   =   *Letters of St. Ignatius of Loyola.* Tr. William J. Young, S.J. (Chicago: Loyola University, 1959).

LW   =   Rahner, Hugo, S.J. *St. Ignatius Loyola: Letters to Women.* Tr. Kathleen Pond and S. A. H. Weetman (New York: Herder and Herder, 1960).

MHSI   =   *Monumenta Historica Societatis Iesu* (Madrid-Rome: 1894-).

OC   =   *San Ignacio de Loyola: Obras Completas.* Fourth revised edition. Ed. Ignacio Iparraguirre, S.I., and Candido de Dalmases, S.I. (Madrid: Biblioteca de Autores Cristianos, 1982).

PY   =   Brodrick, James, S.J. *Saint Ignatius Loyola: The Pilgrim Years 1491-1538.* (New York: Farrar, Straus and Cudahy, 1956).

Introduction

[1] See Preface #1 and Appendix I #2.

[2] See, for example, "The Testament of St. Francis," in *St. Francis of Assisi: Writings and Early Biographies*, ed. Marion A. Habig (Chicago: Franciscan Herald, 1973) 67-70.

[3] Gonçalves da Câmara again returned to Rome in May 1558 to attend the first General Congregation called to elect Ignatius' successor. At the congregation he was elected assistant for Portugal to Father Laínez, the new Father General. On July 3, 1559, he left Rome for Portugal to be tutor to the youthful King Sebastian, and died in Lisbon on March 15, 1575.

[4] See his Preface #3.

[5] See Appendix I #4.

[6] For example, in his Preface #2, he appears to say that Ignatius began his narration in September 1553, while in #10 of the text he says that it was already in progress in August 1553. Also, his Preface #5 says that his last meeting with Ignatius was on the eve of his departure. Since he left Rome on October 23, 1555, that would mean that the final meeting had taken place on October 22, but in #99 of the text he seems to indicate that the last meeting with Ignatius was on October 20.

[7] See *IdL* 18; *PY* 25.

[8] See *FD* doc. 32.

[9] For the names and biographies of the members of Ignatius' immediate family, see *FD* 773-94.

[10] See *PY* 24. The cottage, Eguíbar, where Ignatius lived with his nurse, still stands.

[11] *FD* 782. However, *FN* 1:153 n. 5 says that the marriage took place on September 14, 1493. This date seems unlikely since Martín García was born ca. 1478, and if he married in 1493, it would mean that he had married at age fifteen.

[12] See *FD* doc. 48.

[13] *FD* 238.

[14] For a more complete description of the legal proceedings against Ignatius, see *PY* 45-48 or *IL* 21-23.

[15] For an English translation, see *FX* 462-65.

[16] See *FX* 467.

[17] For a description of Ignatius with reference to his appearance, speech, dress, and work, see *FX* 475-82.

[18] For the text of this resignation, see *LIL* 230.

Preface of Father Luis Gonçalves da Câmara

[1] Some details of his life have already been given in Part I of the Introduction.
[2] Juan Alfonso de Polanco was born in Burgos, Spain, on December 24, 1517, and entered the Society in Rome in 1541. He was named secretary of the Society in 1547 and held that position not only during Ignatius' lifetime, but also during the generalates of Diego Laínez and Francis Borgia. He died in Rome on December 20, 1576.
[3] Jerónimo Nadal was born on August 11, 1507, in Palma de Mallorca, and attended the University of Paris at the same time that Ignatius had been there, and was accepted into the Society in Rome on November 23, 1545. From 1548-1551 he was in Sicily; he made his final profession in Rome on March 25, 1552, and was then sent to Spain as Commissar General. He returned to Rome in 1554, then traveled throughout Italy, Germany, and Spain, promulgating the Society's new Constitutions. He died in Rome on April 3, 1580.
[4] In Nadal's Preface to the Latin translation of Gonçalves da Câmara's text (see Appendix I), he says that he had made this request of Ignatius in 1551, but since he spent all of 1551 in Sicily, he must have meant 1552.
[5] Nadal, in his Preface #3, says that upon his return from Spain he learned that nothing had been done on the project. Since Nadal wrote his Preface some six to eleven years after the event, and seems not to have been aware of Gonçalves da Câmara's Preface, it is possible that his memory did not serve him well.
[6] The second rule of *The Rules of Modesty* reads as follows: "The eyes, for the most part, should be kept lowered, and should not be immoderately raised, or allowed to rove from side to side, and when conversing with persons to whom special deference is due, one should not regard him fixedly, but should keep the eyes slightly lowered" (*OC* 89 n. 13).
[7] *FN* 1:330 indicates that there are some who think the Preface was written during the years 1558-1559, when Gonçalves da Câmara was in Rome attending the Society's first General Congregation, or while acting as assistant to the new Father General, Diego Laínez. In 1559 he returned to Portugal to be tutor to young King Sebastian.
[8] The extant Spanish manuscripts of this Preface lack #5 and abruptly end mid-point in the final sentence of #4. The text of #5 as given here is based on the Latin translation of Gonçalves da Câmara's text.

Chapter 1. Pamplona–Loyola: Convalescence and Conversion

[1] It was a custom in the Middle Ages for a person in danger of death, and when no priest was available, to confess his sins to a layperson. Such a confession was never considered sacramental, but it clearly manifested the individual's contrition for sin. Saint Thomas Aquinas allows this practice (see *Summa theologiae. Supplementum*. Quest. 8, art. 2, resp.), and the prayer books of the fifteenth and sixteenth centuries approved this custom.

[2] See *FN* 1:156.

[3] Polanco states this in *FN* 1:157, and this has been the constant tradition among Jesuits.

[4] *IdL* 75 identifies this Magdalena as Ignatius' sister, while *PY* 61 n. 1 calls her his sister-in-law.

[5] See *IL* 40.

[6] From Martín García's will we learn that the surgeon who operated on Ignatius and cared for him was Martín de Iztiola, and that he had been paid ten ducats for his services. See *FN* 1:369 n. 9, or *FD* doc. 116.

[7] For a list of other popular novels that Ignatius might well have read, see *PY* 42 n. 2.

[8] The full title of Ludolph's book is *Vita Jesu Christi e quatuor evangeliis et scriptoribus orthodoxis concinnata per Ludolphum de Saxonia*. See *PY* 64 n. 1.

[9] See *IL* 43.

[10] See Pedro Leturia, S.I., "Notas críticas sobre la dama del Capitán Loyola," *Archivum Historicum Societatis Iesu* 5 (1936) 84-92.

[11] See Felix de Llanos y Torriglia, "El Capitán Iñigo de Loyola y la dama de sus pensamientos," *Razón y Fe* 124 (1941) 33-69.

[12] See *IdL* 13.

[13] See *IL* 45.

[14] *PY* 72 n. 1.

[15] The buildings of Our Lady of the Caves still stand today but they have not housed monks since the early part of the nineteenth century, when the monastery had been secularized. The government sold the property to the Pickman Pottery Works in 1836, and the factory remained there until 1982 when it moved to another location. The Spanish government again acquired the property and now intends to restore the Charterhouse according to its original plans.

Chapter 2. Montserrat: A Knight's Vigil

¹ See *OC* 98 n. 3.
² The original text (*imagen*) is unclear; it is not known whether this was a statue or a picture of our Lady. *IdL* 135 considers it a statue, while *IL* 52 speaks of it as a picture.
³ Sūra 3:47.
⁴ Sūra 19:22-23.
⁵ *IdL* 138 thinks that it was to Pedrola that the Moor had gone. The geographical details provided by Ignatius perfectly describe the approach to Pedrola; the royal highway does not pass through it, but there is a road branching from the highway leading to it.
⁶ Earlier authors have been of the opinion that the place where Ignatius made his purchases was Lérida; modern authors think it was Igualada. Lérida is a city, while Igualada is a large town and, furthermore, Igualada was known for its cloth, and was but a short distance from Montserrat. See *IdL* 141, and *IL* 53-54.
⁷ *PY* 77 n. 2 tallies the miles from Loyola to Igualada.
⁸ *Ejercitatorio de la vida espiritual*; see *IdL* 149-50, and *PY* 84.

Chapter 3. Manresa: Taught By God

¹ Polanco gives these details in his *Summarium* #17. See *FN* 1:160.
² Father Balduin Delange recalled, in 1598, that Ignatius had once told him, in 1551, that he had used such a book at the time of his conversion. See *FN* 1:392 n. 5.
³ The name of the priest assigned to preach at the Seo in 1552 was Juan Boutabi. See *IL* 60.
⁴ Tradition identifies him as Guillermo de Pellarós, O.P. See *FN* 1:394 n. 10.
⁵ The text clearly states that there was a deep hole (*agujero*) in the room, but it is somewhat difficult to imagine a deep hole in the very room where Ignatius was living and, thus, some have interpreted *agujero* to be a large opening or window through which Ignatius was tempted to throw himself (see *IL* 62). Since Ignatius' room, according to the tradition among the Dominicans was on ground level, it is difficult to conceive how jumping from a window but a few feet from the ground would be attempting suicide! Hence, there are those who postulate that next to Ignatius' room were deep excavations, and that he was tempted to jump through the window into

the excavations. (See *St. Ignatius' Own Story*, tr. William J. Young, S.J. [Chicago: Regnery, 1956] 20). Since the Dominican monastery, where Ignatius had once resided, was destroyed in 1860, there is no way of solving this difficulty.

[6] *FN* 1:397 n. 12 suggests that this was Saint Andrew, the apostle, for according to the *Flos sanctorum*, Andrew is supposed to have said that he would not eat until God had granted pardon to a certain Nicholas. Andrew then fasted for five days, after which period an angel came to him and notified him that Nicholas had been pardoned through the apostle's prayers.

[7] *FN* 1:584; in the same place Gonçalves da Câmara also records that Ignatius read a chapter of *The Imitation* each day of his life.

[8] See *Spiritual Journal of Ignatius Loyola, February 2, 1544 to February 27, 1545*, tr. William J. Young, S.J. (Woodstock, Md.: Woodstock College, 1958).

[9] Polanco says (*FN* 1:160) that this vision took place four months after Ignatius' conversion, but since he does not date the time of that conversion there is no way of knowing when this illumination occurred. The chronology in *OC* 41 suggests that it may have been in August or September 1522.

[10] The monastery and church of Saint Paul the Hermit were situated on the banks of the Cardoner and had been under the care of the Cistercians since 1472. In 1700 the monastery was sold to the Jesuits who then rebuilt the house and restored the chapel. In 1767 the Society lost the property by Charles III's decree expelling the Jesuits from his realm. At that time the house went into private hands. See *OC* 108 n. 14.

[11] The name appears as Amigant in *IL* 63-64, but as Amigrant in *OC* 110 n. 22.

[12] See *FN* 1:408 n. 27.

[13] See *OC* 110 n. 20; Ferrer is the modern form of the name.

[14] See *OC* 110 n. 20.

[15] *OC* 110 n. 22 identifies these ladies as Inés Pascual, Angela Amigrant, Micaela Canyelles, Inés Clavera, and Brianda Paguera.

[16] See *FN* 1:81 n. 16.

[17] See *IL* 70.

[18] See *LW* 262-63.

Chapter 4. Jerusalem: Pilgrim in the Holy Land

[1] See *FN* 1:414 n. 2; *OC* 113 n. 1.

[2] *FD* doc. 64.

3 See *PY* 125 n. 4.

4 See *OC* 114 n. 9.

5 See *FN* 1:420 n. 10; *OC* 115 n. 10.

6 See *OC* 115 n. 14.

7 See *FN* 1:420 n. 10.

8 See *FN* 1:420 n. 10; *OC* 115 n. 12; *PY* 125-35; *IL* 80-83. For a full description of what a pilgrimage to the Holy Land was like, see H. F. M. Prescott, *Friar Felix at Large: A Fifteenth-Century Pilgrimage to the Holy Land* (New Haven: Yale University, 1950). Friar Felix made two pilgrimages: one in 1480 and another in 1483. Though his pilgrimages preceded that of Ignatius by fifty years, nevertheless, the vicissitudes of the pilgrim in the Holy Land had hardly changed.

9 See *FN* 1:422 n. 11; *PY* 135-43; *IL* 83-84.

10 See *PY* 143 n. 2.

11 *OC* 118 n. 21 states that Christians of the Girdle was the name given to Syrian Christians who worked at the Franciscan monastery of Mount Sion in Jerusalem. The presupposition is that the girdle they wore somehow identified them as Christians, otherwise, why be known as Christians of the Girdle. Prescott (*Friar Felix at Large* p. 190) speaks of Christians of the Girdle but does not distinguish them by the girdle they wore but says, "the Christians of the Girdle dress in Saracen fashion except that, instead of the white turban, they wear one of bright or dark blue."

Chapter 5. Cyprus–Genoa: The Pilgrim's Return

1 See *FN* 1:428 n. 1; *PY* 145.

2 We are here following the opinion of C. Dalmases as found in *FN* 1:428 n. 1. Some authors, e.g., Dudon (*IL* 85-88), have Ignatius traveling with Füssli, and thus they describe in detail the storms the *Malipiera* encountered and the ports where it sought refuge. There is one omission which these authors fail to consider, namely, Ignatius explicitly says that his ship landed in Apulia, but the Füssli account has no mention of any landing in Apulia. Furthermore, Ignatius calls his vessel small, while the *Malipiera* was certainly not small.

3 See *FN* 2:433 n. 29; *OC* 114 n. 7 and n. 9.

4 Though the text gives his name as Portundo, it was actually Portuondo. See *OC* 121 n. 8.

Chapter 6. Barcelona and Alcalá: Student Days

[1] See *OC* 121 n. 1; however *FN* 1:440 n. 8 says that Lent began on February 10.

[2] She was Ignatius' benefactor, not only during his days in Barcelona but also later during his years of study in Paris. In 1543 she came to Rome and in 1545 took vows in the Society of Jesus, but because of ensuing difficulties Ignatius dispensed her from those vows. She returned to Barcelona in 1547 and entered the Franciscan convent of Santa Maria de Jerusalén, where she died in 1554. For further details, see *LW* 262-95.

[3] *IL* 94 suggests that this monk may have been Alfonso de Guerreto and that he may have been a victim of the plague that desolated that area during August-September of 1523. José M. March is of a different opinion in his "Quién y de dónde era el monje manresano, amigo de San Ignacio de Loyola," *Estudios Ecclesiasticos* 4 (1925) 185-93.

[4] Ardévol began teaching at the *Estudio General* in Barcelona in 1525. See *OC* 121 n. 3, and C. Dalmases, S.I., "Los estudios de San Ignacio en Barcelona (1524-1526)," *Archivum Historicum Societatis Iesu* 10 (1941) 283-93.

[5] Tradition has it that when Ignatius left Montserrat and was on his way to Manresa, he met the widow Pascual, also returning from Montserrat. In answer to his question where he could find a hospital that would give him lodging, she directed him to that of Saint Lucy. Ignatius' earliest extant letter was written to her. She died in 1548. For further details, see *LW* 173-84.

[6] Calixto de Sa may have been born in Segovia, and before he attached himself to Ignatius he made a pilgrimage to the Holy Land, probably in 1524. After Ignatius went to Paris in 1528, Calixto intended to follow but then changed his mind. He twice visited Mexico and returned a wealthy man settling down in Salamanca. See *FN* 1:171 n. 10.

[7] Lope de Cáceres was born in Segovia and had been in the service of the Viceroy of Catalonia. After Ignatius moved to Paris he returned to Segovia. See *FN* 1:170 n. 9.

[8] Juan de Arteaga was born in Estepa, and remained with Ignatius until the latter moved to Paris. In 1540 Pope Paul III appointed him Bishop of Chiapa in Mexico. He arrived ill in Veracruz and went to Mexico City to recuperate, but he died there on September 8, 1541, and was buried in that city's cathedral. See *FN* 1:170 n. 8.

[9] See *FN* 1:440 n. 8; *OC* 123 n. 8.

[10] He became Archbishop of Toledo in 1495, and as archbishop he financed the printing of many religious books, the most famous of which was the

polyglot Bible, *Complutensis*, in six volumes (1514-1517). It contained the first printed text of the Greek New Testament. He died in 1517.

11 The hospital was founded in 1483 by Luis de Antezana, a gentleman-in-waiting of the Catholic Kings. The exact identity of this individual is uncertain, but he was either Lope de Deza or Juan Vázquez. See *FN* 1:439 n. 7; *OC* 123 n. 7.

12 See *FN* 1:418 n. 5.

13 Domingo Soto (1494-1560) had been a professor at Alcalá before he entered the Dominican Order in 1524. His text on logic, *Summulae*, was first printed in Burgos in 1529, but an earlier manuscript version of it could have been in use at Alcalá when Ignatius was there.

14 St. Albert the Great's (c. 1200-1280) *Physicorum libri VIII* was his extended commentary on Aristotle's natural philosophy and was written between 1245-1248.

15 Peter Lombard's (c. 1095-1160) *Sententiarum libri IV* was completed about 1157. It was a systematic presentation of scholastic theology, and because the book had become the favorite theological text of the Middle Ages Peter became familiarly known as the Master of the Sentences.

16 The original text gives the family name as Guía. Diego de Eguía was born in Estella in Navarre and on his mother's side was related to Francis Xavier. He joined Ignatius in Venice in January 1537, pronounced his vows in Rome on February 22, 1542, and died there on June 16, 1556, just weeks before Ignatius' own death. Diego's brother Esteban also joined Ignatius in Venice in 1537, and died in Rome on January 28, 1551. See *FN* 1:110 n. 3; *OC* 124 n. 13.

17 In 1525, and again in 1526, Miguel printed a Spanish translation of Erasmus' *Enchiridion militis christiani*, and it is probable that it was through these editions that Ignatius made his first contact with Erasmus.

18 The two inquisitors from Toledo were Miguel Carrasco and Alonso Mejía. See *OC* 125 n. 17; *FN* 1:443 n. 18.

19 Figueroa was the Archbishop of Toledo's vicar general in Alcalá. Later Charles V appointed him Regent of the Kingdom of Naples and he served as President of the Council of Castile. He was always friendly toward Ignatius and died in Madrid on March 23, 1565.

20 The documents of these Alcalá investigations may be found in *FD* 319-49. A very good resumé is in *PY* 174-79.

21 Jean Reynalde had been a page in the service of Martín de Córdoba, Viceroy of Navarre. He went to Alcalá to begin studies, and being wounded in a student brawl was taken to the Antezana Hospital where he got to know Ignatius. Upon recovery, he asked to become one of Ignatius' group.

22 Her husband was the treasurer of Castile, and she was known for her

charity and devotion to the Blessed Sacrament.

[23] *FN* 1:174.

[24] See *FN* 1:448 n. 26; *OC* 127 n. 26.

[25] *FN* 1:448 n. 27 indicates that the ladies appeared before Figueroa on May 21, 1527. One wonders why the sentence freeing Ignatius was only given on June 1?

[26] See *FD* 340-42.

[27] Ignatius speaks of four years of study, but Figueroa's sentence demanded only three (see *FN* 1:450 n. 31).

[28] He became Archbishop of Toledo in 1524 and died in 1534. He was a great patron of learning and was an acquaintance of Erasmus to whom he granted an annual pension of 200 gold ducats. In return, Erasmus dedicated his edition of Augustine's works to him. The archbishop was visiting Valladolid for the baptism of the son of Charles V, the future Philip II, who was born on May 21, 1527.

Chapter 7. Salamanca: On Trial

[1] In the Spanish text, the word we have translated as group is *compañía.* This is somewhat interesting because *Compañía* is the name that Ignatius and the first Jesuits chose as their name in 1537. By calling his Alcalá-Salamanca friends *compañía,* did Ignatius think of these men as the first beginnings of the *Compañía de Jesús*?

[2] See *OC* 129 n. 1.

[3] Erasmus of Rotterdam (1446-1536) was the most celebrated humanist of his day. His adversaries claimed he attacked the basic institutions of the Church and prepared the way for Luther.

[4] The conference began on June 27 and ended on August 13, 1527. At this conference the Dominicans and Franciscans manifested themselves as Erasmus' most bitter opponents. Though twenty-one propositions were excerpted from Erasmus' writings, the theologians at the conference only discussed the first two, and since the participants were unable to come to any agreement, the Grand Inquisitor suspended the conference without passing any judgment on Erasmus.

[5] Polanco says that the room was dark and "had a great number of different kinds of animals" (*FN* 1:175-76).

[6] As the bishop's representative Frías had attended the conference on Erasmus in Valladolid (see *FN* 1:456 n. 5), and later taught Scripture and theology at the University of Salamanca. ˙

7 See *FN* 1:458 n. 6.

8 See *OC* 130 n. 7; *FN* 1:458 n. 7.

9 Mendoza was born in 1508 and became a cardinal in 1545. He was transferred to the see of Burgos in 1550 and died in 1566.

10 See *FN* 2:137-38.

Chapter 8. Paris: University Studies and First Companions

1 *PY* 208 suggests that Ignatius' route to Paris may have been as follows: Barcelona, Perpignan, Narbonne, Carcassone, Toulouse, Cahors, Limoges, Bourges, Orléans, and finally Paris.

2 Writing to Inés Pascual on March 3, 1528, Ignatius says: "Favored by the weather and in perfect health, by the grace and goodness of God our Lord, I arrived in this city of Paris, where I shall continue my studies until it please the Lord to ordain otherwise, on the second day of February" (*LW* 180).

3 The college was founded in the fourteenth century and was named after Gilles Aycelin de Montaigu, Archbishop of Rouen. It was located on Paris' left bank and among its more famous students were Erasmus, Rabelais, and Calvin who had left the college just a few days before Ignatius arrived. The college building is no longer standing; in its place is the Bibliothèque Sainte-Geneviève, near the Pantheon.

4 The hospital, located on the right bank, was founded in the fourteenth century. Neither the hospital nor the church of the Holy Innocents remain today; the site of the former hospital is today's 133 Rue Saint-Denis.

5 Juan Castro was born in Burgos, Spain, in 1485. When Ignatius got to know him he was teaching at the Sorbonne and working towards his doctorate in theology which he received in 1532. He returned to Spain and in 1535 entered the Charterhouse of Val de Cristo near Segorbe, and Ignatius visited him there, as he mentions in #90. In 1542 Castro became prior of the Charterhouse of Porta Coeli in Valencia and died there in 1556. Val de Cristo remained a monastery until 1834 when it was suppressed by the government. The buildings are now in ruins. Porta Coeli still exists as a monastery. See *OC* 134 n. 7, and *FX* 137 n. 240.

6 Juan Luís Vives was born in Valencia, Spain, in 1492. He studied in Paris and in 1519 became professor of humanities at Louvain and became friendly with Erasmus. He taught at Corpus Christi College, Oxford, and received

a Doctor of Laws from that same institution. He became court counselor, private secretary to Queen Catherine, and education advisor to Henry VIII. He died in Bruges in 1540. For Ignatius' dinner with him, see *FN* 2:557.

[7] See n. 5. above.

[8] Pedro de Peralta came from the diocese of Toledo and received his master's degree in 1529. After attempting to make a pilgrimage to the Holy Land he returned to Toledo and became a canon at the cathedral and a famous preacher. He always retained his affection for Ignatius and the Society. See *OC* 135 n. 9.

[9] Not much is known about Amador de Elduayen except that he came from Guipúzcoa and had matriculated at the university in 1526. See *OC* 135 n. 9; *FX* 138 n. 242.

[10] Diogo de Gouvea (c. 1471-1557), a Portuguese, governed Collège de Sainte-Barbe from 1520 to 1548. See *OC* 136 n. 10.

[11] For more on this seamless robe of Christ, see Joan Carroll Cruz, *Relics* (Huntington, Ind.: Our Sunday Visitor, 1984) 23-27.

[12] Doña Leonor Mascarenhas (1503-1584) was a noble Portuguese who had come to Spain with Infanta Isabella when the latter married Charles V in 1526. She remained as a lady-in-waiting and served as governess to the young Philip II. Ignatius may have met her when he went to visit Archbishop Fonseca in Valladolid in 1527. See *OC* 138 n. 15. For further details of her life, see *LW* 417-33.

[13] At the time of Calixto's first visit to Mexico he was only twenty-four or twenty-five years old. The "spiritually-inclined lady" that Ignatius mentions was Catalina Hernández, a native of Salamanca. See *OC* 140 n. 16.

[14] The original text identifies the poison as *acqua di solimano* (Spanish *agua de solimán*). *Solimán* means "corrosive sublimate" but its chemical make-up is mercuric chloride.

[15] It has been suggested that it was Dr. Pedro Ortiz (1501-1548) who brought the accusation against Ignatius before the Inquisition. He lived at Montaigu and had been Peralta's patron. In 1529 Ortiz went to Salamanca to teach Scripture and from the end of 1530 he represented Charles V in Rome in regard to Henry VIII's request for a divorce. In Rome Ortiz and Ignatius became close friends and Ignatius took him through the Exercises, as he mentions in #98. See *FX* 139 n. 245.

[16] Matthieu Ory, O.P., was a Breton who received his doctorate in 1526 and then taught theology in the Dominican monastery of Saint-Jacques. He became prior of his monastery in 1535 and died in 1557. See *FX* 249 n. 16.

[17] The college was founded in 1460 and had Saint Barbara as its patron. Of the medieval collegiate structures in Paris it is one of the few still stand-

ing; its entrance today is 4 Rue Valette, near the Pantheon.

[18] Juan Peña came from the diocese of Sigüenza, Spain. He received his master's degree in 1525 and taught philosophy at Sainte-Barbe while he continued his studies in medicine. See *OC* 141 n. 21.

[19] Pierre Favre was born in Villaret, Savoy, France, on April 13, 1506, went to Paris in 1525 and received his licentiate degree in March 1530. He was ordained to the priesthood on May 30, 1534, and celebrated his first Mass on July 22, 1534. As a Jesuit he traveled widely making the Society known in Italy, Germany, and Spain. He returned to Rome and died there on August 1, 1546. On September 5, 1872, Pope Pius IX, acknowledging the cult that had been paid to Faber in his native land of Savoy, confirmed it by apostolic decree and declared that he was among the blessed in heaven. His feast day is celebrated on August 2.

[20] Francisco de Jassu y Javier was born in Navarre, Spain, on April 7, 1506. He went to Paris in 1525 and received his licentiate degree in 1530 and began teaching philosophy at Collège de Dormans-Beauvais (1530). Francis arrived in Rome in 1538 and in 1540 was appointed to the Society's mission in India. He left Portugal in April 1541 and arrived in Goa in May 1542. As a missionary Xavier labored in India, Malaya, and Japan, and was waiting to enter China when he died on December 3, 1552. Xavier was declared blessed by Pope Paul V on October 25, 1619, and canonized by Pope Gregory XV on March 12, 1622. His feast is celebrated on December 3.

[21] Simón Rodrigues was born of noble parents in 1510 in the village of Vouzella in the diocese of Viseu in northern Portugal. He was first educated in Lisbon, then came to Paris in 1527 and studied at Collège de Sainte-Barbe. In his career as a Jesuit he was superior (1540-1546) and provincial (1546-1552) of the Portuguese province. In 1553 he was called to Italy where he remained until 1564 when he went to Spain. In 1573 he returned to Portugal and died there in 1579.

[22] Diego Laínez was born in 1512 in Almazán, Spain. He attended the University of Alcalá, arriving there after Ignatius had left for Salamanca. He earned his master's degree at Alcalá in 1532, and then began his study of theology. He went to Paris in 1533 to meet Ignatius. Later in life Laínez served as papal theologian at the Council of Trent (1546, 1551, and 1562). He was named provincial of Italy in 1552, made vicar general on the death of Ignatius in 1556, and was elected Ignatius' successor as general in 1558. He died in 1565.

[23] Alfonso Salmerón was born on September 6, 1515, in Toledo. He went to Alcalá to study and there he met Diego Laínez. Together they went to Paris to find Ignatius. Salmerón was papal theologian at the Council of Trent (1546, 1551, and 1562), and was provincial of the Naples prov-

ince from 1558-1576. He died in Naples in 1585.

[24] Nicolas Bobadilla's true name was Nicolás Alonso y Pérez, but he is known as Bobadilla because it was there that he was born about 1509. He studied at Valladolid, then went to Alcalá where he earned his bachelor's degree in 1529. He returned to Valladolid to teach logic while he studied theology for four years. He decided to go to Paris to study Latin, Greek, and Hebrew, and arrived there in the fall of 1533 when he met Ignatius. As a Jesuit he proved to be a tireless worker: in Germany (1542-1548), in Italy (1548-1558), in Valtellina (1558-1559), in Dalmatia (1559-1561), in Italy (1561-1590). He died in Loreto in 1590, the last of the first Jesuits.

[25] Jerónimo Frago y Gárces was born in Uncastillo in the diocese of Pamplona. He received his master's degree in Paris in 1521, taught philosophy 1521-1525, and in 1529 began teaching Scripture at the Sorbonne. He received his doctor's degree in 1533 and died as a canon in Pamplona in 1537.

[26] So widespread was the plague during the summer of 1533 that Parlement issued ordinances on September 13 dealing with the problem. See *FX* 191.

[27] See *PY* 275 n. 2.

[28] See *OC* 144 n. 24.

[29] See *IL* 142.

[30] See *OC* 144 n. 24.

[31] See *FD* doc. 84.

[32] *PY* 276-77 identifies Ignatius' trouble as "biliary calculus, or chronic cholecystitis associated with gall stones." There Brodrick gives a quotation from Realdo Colombo, the surgeon who embalmed Ignatius shortly after his death, in which the surgeon states that he had taken from Ignatius' body numberless stones of various colors found in the kidneys, lungs, liver, and portal vein. See also Hugo Rahner, *Ignatius: The Man and the Priest* (Rome: Centrum Ignatianum Spiritualitatis, 1977) 99-105 where he treats Ignatius' physical ailments.

[33] The crypt of Saint-Denis, 9 Rue Antionette, is now cared for by the Auxiliatrices.

[34] Text of this decree may be found in *FD* doc. 86. For English translation, see *PY* 278.

[35] See *OC* 147 n. 30.

Chapter 9. Spain: A Return Visit Home

[1] *PY* 305 suggests that after leaving Paris, Ignatius passed through Chartres, Tours, Poitiers, Angoulême, and Bordeaux before reaching Bayonne.

The distance from Paris to Azpeitia would be about 550 miles, and would have taken him about a month to traverse.

2 Neither *OC* nor *FN* identify the individual who recognized Ignatius in Bayonne; however, *IL* 158 identifies him as Juan de Eguíbar, a supplier of meat to the markets in Azpeitia.

3 When Francis Borgia came to Azpeitia in January 1552, he stopped at this same hospice and found, sixteen years later, that the horse was still there. The horse is described as a nag (*cuartago*), "very fat and in good condition" (*OC* 148 n. 3; *FN* 1:482 n. 3).

4 See *IL* 167.

5 These ordinances may be found in *FD* doc. 88.

6 Ignatius' brother, Martín García, left a legacy in his will for the bell ringers, so that the bells may continue to be rung daily for this intention. See *FN* 1:486 n. 8.

7 In his letter (August-September 1540) to the citizens of Azpeitia Ignatius reminds them to do without card playing and that there should be a prohibition on the sale of playing cards. See *LIL* 44.

8 In the same letter Ignatius asks the citizenry of Azpeitia to put an end to the abuse of women wearing the headdress of the married when these women are not actually married (see *LIL* 44). In his letter (September 1539) to his nephew Beltrán, who succeeded Martín García as master of Loyola, Ignatius asks him to continue to see to the reform of the clergy especially in Azpeitia since that parish church was under the patronage of the Loyola family. See *LIL* 39.

9 See *OC* 150 n. 7.

10 See *OC* 150 n. 7.

11 Of the four Spaniards in his group, Ignatius visited the relatives of three of them (Xavier, Salmerón, and Laínez), but it seems that he did not visit that of Bobadilla. Bobadilla's father had died in 1517, and *IL* 178 suggests that perhaps his mother was also dead by this time.

12 See *FN* 1:186 n. 12.

13 Khird was a Barbary pirate and had adopted the name "Khair ed-Din" as a honorific title. He became admiral of the sultan's fleet in 1533 and died in 1546.

14 See *FN* 1:188 n. 10.

15 See *FN* 1:188 n. 13.

Chapter 10. Venice and Vicenza: Awaiting Passage to the Holy Land

1 On February 12, 1536, Ignatius wrote to Jaime Cassador, archdeacon

of the cathedral of Barcelona, to inform him that he had been in Venice
for a month and a half and that he was enjoying the hospitality and friend-
ship of a very good and learned man (see *LIL* 15). In this letter Ignatius
does not identify his host, but both *PY* 321 and *FX* 300 think it was Lippomani, while *IL* 183 thinks it may have been Martín de Zornoza, the
Spanish consul in Venice.

2 Pietro Contarini was procurator at the hospital for the incurably ill in
Venice. In 1557 he was appointed Bishop of Paphos in Cyprus, and resigned
that see in 1562. Together with Cardinal Gasparo Contarini, a relative of
his, he was of great assistance to the young Society. He died in Padua in
1563. See *OC* 152 n. 1.

3 Gasparo de Dotti's name appears in the original text as de Doctis, that
is, in its Latin form. When he became acquainted with Ignatius, he was
connected with the papal legate in Venice, Girolamo Verallo. In 1551 he
was made governor of Loreto, and in 1556 was permitted to take simple
vows in the Society while remaining, at Ignatius' recommendation, in charge
of the sanctuary. He died in Loreto in 1563. See *OC* 152 n. 2; *FX* 304 n. 79.

4 *OC* 153 n. 3 indicates that it is not certain who this individual was, but
following *FN* 1:490 n. 3 it suggests that it might have been a certain Rodrigo
Rozas.

5 Diego de Hoces was born in Málaga, and was in Venice because he had
only recently returned from the Holy Land. His death in March 1538 may
have been the result of his caring for the plague-stricken. See *OC* 153 n.
4; *PY* 324 n. 1.

6 The text refers to a Bishop of Cette, but since there is no diocese by
that name some have suggested that it should be Ceuta in Mauretania, but
this is unlikely (see *OC* 154 n. 5). More probably the name should be Chieti,
for its former bishop, Gian Pietro Carafa, was then residing in Venice. In
1524, together with St. Cajetan of Theine, Carafa founded the Congregation of Clerks Regular. Carafa was the congregation's first superior and
because he had been Bishop of Chieti (*Theate* in Latin) members of the congregation became known as Theatines. During the sack of Rome in 1527,
the Theatines were banished and found refuge in Venice where Carafa remained until September 1536, when he was called to Rome. On December
22 of that year Pope Paul III made him a cardinal.

7 The actual reason for Carafa's animosity toward Ignatius has never been
uncovered. Sometime in 1536, Ignatius wrote him a letter in which he
politely offered suggestions on how Carafa's congregation could better itself.
It is presumed that Ignatius' sincere observations were not well received.
Carafa might have viewed the letter as from someone, who was his junior,
attempting to tell him, the senior, how the Theatine congregation should

be managed. Furthermore, Ignatius was not only not yet ordained, but he was not even a member of any religious congregation, nor did he have any thoughts of founding a congregation of his own. (For a copy of this letter of Ignatius see *LIL* 28-31). On the death of Pope Marcellus II in 1555, Carafa, then in his seventy-ninth year, was elected to the papacy on May 23 and took the name Paul IV. When Ignatius heard this news it is said that his jaw fell and he immediately went to chapel to pray. When he returned he appeared as happy as if his closest friend had been elected pope.

[8] "Venetiis excitata est contradictio a Petro Caraffa." See *Epistolae Hieronymi Nadal* 4 (*MHSI*) (Madrid: Lopez del Horno, 1905) 706.

[9] This sentence was given on October 13, 1537, and is doc. 105 in *FD*.

[10] Claude Jay was born between 1500-1504. As a youth he attended school with Faber at Collège de la Roche, Savoy. He was ordained a priest on March 28, 1528, and was conducting a small school when Faber visited him in 1533 and encouraged him to go to Paris to continue his studies. He arrived in Paris in October 1534, made the Exercises under Faber's direction and pronounced his vows at Montmartre on August 15, 1535. As a Jesuit he labored in Italy (1537-1541) and in Germany (1542-1549). He attended the Council of Trent (1545-1547) and the Diet of Augsburg (1550). He died in Vienna in 1552 as rector of the university in that city. See *FX* 260.

[11] Paschase Broët was born in Picardy in 1500. He studied at Amiens and was ordained there in 1524. He spent the next ten years in a parish but then went to Paris in 1534. There he met Faber, made the Exercises, and pronounced his vows at Montmartre on August 15, 1536. As a Jesuit he labored in Siena (1537-1540), went with Salmerón as papal legate to Ireland (1541), and then labored in Italy (1542-1551). He was provincial in France (1552-1562) and died in Paris in 1562 while serving the plague-stricken. See *FX* 261-62.

[12] Jean Codure came from southern France and was born in 1508. He came to Paris and began his studies at the university in 1534. He placed himself under Faber's spiritual direction, made the Exercises, and took vows with Broët at Montmartre on August 15, 1536. Codure was the first of the companions to die in Rome; he died on August 29, 1541. See *FX* 263.

[13] Of the two brothers, Esteban was the elder and a widower, while Diego was already ordained. Both brothers set out for Spain before the companions began their work in Venice's hospitals. See n. 16 under chap. 6 above.

[14] Ortiz was the individual who had denounced Ignatius to the Inquisition in Paris over the Castro-Peralta affair (see #81). He had been in Rome since the end of 1530 as Charles V's agent assigned to defend the rights of the emperor's aunt, Queen Catherine, against Henry VIII's attempt to divorce her. After the queen had died on January 7, 1536, Pope Paul III asked him

to remain in Rome as a special counselor.

[15] See *OC* 155 n. 8.

[16] Verallo was born about 1497 and had been nuncio in Venice from 1537 to February 1540. He became a cardinal on April 8, 1549, and died on October 10, 1555.

[17] See *OC* 155 n. 8; *FX* 347.

[18] See *OC* 156 n. 10.

[19] *PY* 348. n. 1 suggests that they were given only hard moldy crusts which they had to boil in order to make them edible.

[20] See *FX* 360.

[21] Codure had been in Treviso with Hoces. It seems that they had received word of Rodrigues' relapse (after Ignatius' visit), and feeling that Hoces could do more for Rodrigues than Jay, who knew no Portuguese, Hoces went to Bassano to be with them. Rather than remaining alone in Bassano, Codure went on to Vicenza. See *FX* 360 n. 194.

[22] See *FN* 2:84.

[23] See *FN* 2:133.

[24] See *FX* 492.

Chapter 11. Rome: First Year in the Eternal City

[1] The house, though now remodeled and enlarged, still stands on Via San Sebastianello 11. See *FX* 408 n. 11.

[2] See *FX* 415 n. 55.

[3] Francisco Estrada was a Spaniard, born about 1519 in Dueñas. He had studied in Alcalá and then went to Rome in 1536 to seek his fortune. Doctor Ortiz secured a position for him in the household of Cardinal Gian Pietro Carafa. While Ignatius was in Monte Cassino Cardinal Carafa dismissed the Spaniards in his household and, thus, Estrada was on his way to Naples hoping to enlist in the Spanish forces. Having met Ignatius, he returned to Rome. As a Jesuit he was a renowned preacher in Italy, Belgium, Portugal, and Spain; he was rector at Burgos (1551-1554) and provincial (1554-1557). His health then began to fail and he spent his last fifteen years living as a hermit in Toledo where he died in 1584. See *FX* 417 n. 65; *OC* 160 n. 3.

[4] Cardinal Contarini (1483-1542) was made cardinal in 1535, and had served as papal legate to Spire (1540), Germany (1541), Bologna (1542), and to the emperor (1542). It was he who showed the Formula of the Institute to Paul III.

[5] For a thorough description of this persecution and the role that Mainar-

di's sermons played in it, see *FX* 419-42.

⁶ See *FX* 421-22; *OC* 161 n. 7.

⁷ Ignatius describes this persecution in his letter of September 18, 1538, to Isabel Roser. See *LW* 269-74.

⁸ Miguel Landívar was, at one time, Francis Xavier's servant in Paris, and when Ignatius converted Xavier from his worldly ways, Miguel nurtured so great a hatred for Ignatius that he resolved to murder him, but failed in the attempt. He was in Venice in 1536 and went with the companions to Rome in 1537, but soon after left them. He appeared in Rome once more in 1538, this time as Ignatius' accuser and was banished. See *FX* 188 n. 265.

⁹ Conversini was, since 1537, Bishop of Bertinoro. Before Paul III left Rome for Nice, March 1538, the pope appointed him governor and judge of Rome. See *FX* 423 n. 123.

¹⁰ For this letter see *Epistolae mixtae ex variis Europae locis ab anno 1537 ad 1556 scriptae* 1: *1537-1548 (MHSI)*. (Madrid: Aurial, 1898) 11-14.

¹¹ The cardinal became papal legate in Rome when Paul III set out for Nice.

¹² This sentence may be found in *FD* doc. 108.

¹³ *Spiritual Journal of Ignatius Loyola, February 2, 1544 to February 27, 1545,* tr. William J. Young, S.J. (Woodstock, Md.: Woodstock College, 1958).

Appendix I. Preface of Father Nadal

¹ This is a translation of the Latin text that appears in *FN* 1:354-63; it appears at the bottom of those pages. A Spanish translation of the same appears in *OC* 85-86. The substance of these notes has been taken from the notes that accompany the Spanish translation.

² The Society of Jesus received the official confirmation of Pope Paul III on September 27, 1540; the book of the Spiritual Exercises was approved by the same pope on July 31, 1548; and Ignatius completed writing the Society's Constitutions.

³ *OC* 87 n. 3 suggests that the date should be 1552 since Nadal spent all of 1551 in Sicily and only returned to Rome on January 5, 1552.

⁴ At this time Polanco was Ignatius' secretary.

⁵ Ponce de Cogordan was a Frenchman who entered the Society as a priest in 1541, made his solemn profession in Rome in 1553, was treasurer of the Jesuit community in Rome and was back in Paris by 1560. He died there in 1582.

⁶ According to *OC* 88 n. 5 this should be 1553. After making his profession in Rome on March 25, 1552, Nadal was again sent to Sicily. In January

1553 he was once more in Rome, and then in April of that year he set out for Spain and Portugal to promulgate the Society's Constitutions among the Jesuits in those countries.

[7] Nadal wrote this Preface between 1561 and 1576, and evidently had forgotten that Ignatius had begun to narrate his life to Gonçalves da Câmara in August-September 1553.

[8] The first General Congregation, which elected Father Laínez General of the Society, took place in 1558.

[9] Annibal du Coudret, a Frenchman, was born in 1525, entered the Society in 1546; was sent to Sicily in 1548 and returned to Rome in 1558. While stationed at the Roman College he translated Gonçalves da Câmara's Spanish-Italian text into Latin. In 1561 he returned to France and died at Avignon in 1599.